CULTURES OF THE WORLD
Egypt

Cavendish
Square
New York

Published in 2015 by Cavendish Square Publishing, LLC
243 5th Avenue, Suite 136, New York, NY 10016

Library of Congress Cataloging-in-Publication Data
Pateman, Robert, 1954- author.
 Egypt / Robert Pateman, Salwa El-Hamamsy, Josie Elias.
    pages cm. — (Cultures of the world)
 ISBN 978-0-7614-4992-8 (hardcover) ISBN 978-0-76147-992-5 (ebook)
 1. Egypt—Juvenile literature. I. El-Hamamsy, Salwa. II. Elias, Josie. III. Title. IV. Series: Cultures of the world.

DT49.P382 2014
962—dc23

2014007389

Writers: Robert Pateman/Salwa El-Hamamsy; Deborah Nevins—3rd ed.
Editorial Director Third Edition: Dean Miller
Editor Third Edition: Deborah Nevins
Art Director, Third Edition: Jeffrey Talbot
Designer Third Edition: Jessica Nevins
Production Manager: Jennifer Ryder-Talbot
Production Editor: David McNamara
Picture Researcher Third Edition: Jessica Nevins

PRECEDING PAGE
A young camel in the desert.

Printed in the United States of America

CONTENTS

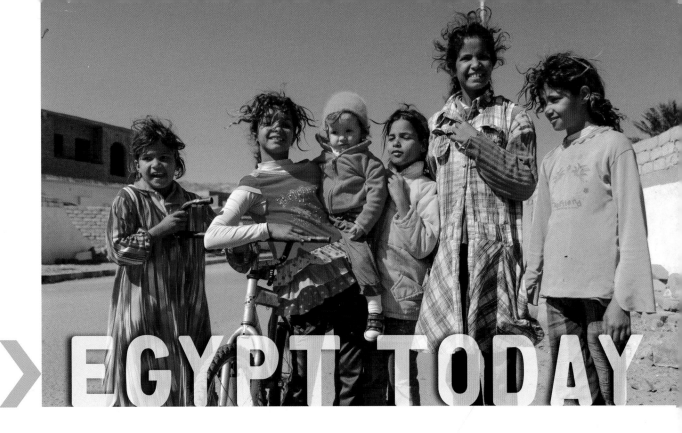

EGYPT TODAY

EGYPT IS A LAND OF WONDERS—A PLACE OF MYSTERY, BEAUTY, epic history, and political struggle. Located on the northeast corner of the African continent, Egypt is at once a Mediterranean country, an African country, a Middle Eastern country—and in many ways, a country unlike any other. Its very location, where Africa touches Asia, places it at the crossroads of East and West. Isolated in ancient times by its geography, it would ultimately become the center of momentous historical movements and change. It is a land of stark contrasts and puzzling contradictions: wet and dry, old and new, consistency and transformation.

The geography of the area sets the tone for these contradictions. It covers a vast expanse, but its people are crammed onto a narrow strip of livable land. The fertile, green valley of the Nile River, which sustains life, dissects an immense territory of nearly lifeless sand desert. In fact, the line between the two environments is abrupt. Egypt is a ribbon of green running through a canvas of beige. Dotted throughout the deserts, however, are several oases—mystifying green islands of life.

Egypt's history dates to the dawn of humankind. Paleolithic (Stone Age) peoples hunted, gathered, and made tools in the Nile Valley for many thousands of years. And then, around 5,000 years ago, a civilization emerged which today is called Pharaonic, or Dynastic Egypt. This civilization lasted 3,000 years—1,000 years longer than the span of time from the birth of Jesus Christ until today!

This was Ancient Egypt. (Of course, at the time, the people did not consider themselves to be ancient. They lived in the "now" of their own times.) These were the people who built the pyramids—monuments that are amazing even by today's standards, and astonishing in the context of when they were built. These were the people who buried their kings in tombs filled with art: objects of gold and other metals, precious stones, limestone, and other materials that would last over the long sweep of time. The statuary and paintings, along with everyday artifacts, were not placed in the tombs for decorative purposes. In fact, they were not intended to be seen at all; not by human eyes, that is. The tombs were equipped with everything the

In this wall painting dating to the Fifth Dynasty (2500-2350 BCE), a man stirs batter for bread making.

deceased might need in the afterlife. All of the contents were designed to smooth the dead person's passage into the next realm. These objects tell rich stories that reveal the details of those ancient lives. Paintings and wall reliefs dazzle with images of gods and kings, masters and slaves; wars and peace; food and comfort; births, deaths, and the daily work of living.

The people of the Nile Valley worshiped deities that ruled the realms of nature. Ra, the sun god, was swallowed every night by the sky goddess, Nut, and was then reborn every morning. Shu, the god of the air, held up Nut with his arms. Other deities represented the forces of life and death—Ma'at, the goddess of truth, justice, and harmony; Seth, the god of evil and chaos; Amun, the god of creation. These spirit gods lived invisibly among the mortals and could be accessed at sacred sites. Through this complex mythology, the ancient people made sense of their lives. They developed a concept of time and created calendars to mark its passage. And millennium after millennium, the Nile flooded and flowed and brought life to Egypt. But the winds that blew across the waves of desert sand—and across the reaches of time—also blew in waves of change.

Today's Egyptians are proud of their extraordinary heritage, but they are also modern people facing the challenges of the twenty-first century.

The Isis Temple reflects in the waters of Lake Nasser. When the Aswan Dam was built in 1971, it flooded the region and created this human-made lake. The temple and its island were submerged. An international effort headed by UNESCO created a new island, and salvaged and rebuilt the temple, block by block.

It has proven lately to be a difficult time. Egypt is an Arab nation that also looks to the West. Islam provides the values and traditions guiding personal behavior, family life, and social interaction. The West inspires technological advancement and entices with its popular culture. It also encourages new ways of thinking about personal freedoms and democracy.

This has created a tension demonstrated by something of a generational conflict. Three out of four Egyptians are under forty, and more than two out of three are under thirty-five. The younger generation is tweeting, blogging, and texting about new ideas while the older generation holds on to political power. In 2011, popular protests forced President Hosni Mubarak from office. The demonstrations were a signal that younger Egyptians intend to make a change in their country. However, the outcome has been rocky as Egypt struggles with differences of opinion about what form a new government should take. One faction, the Muslim Brotherhood, favors a stronger Islamic influence in government. Another group wants a more secular, or nonreligious, democratic government.

These sorts of upheavals are not confined to Egypt. Most of the Arab world

The Nile River flows through the modern city of Cairo, the capital of Egypt.

is in turmoil, facing similar conflicts to greater or lesser degrees. Social change often comes about with such turbulence. The problem for Egypt is that the unrest has greatly impacted tourism, one of the most important parts of Egypt's economy.

But meanwhile, Egyptian lives go on. People go to school or work, enjoy their families, play games, celebrate happy occasions, and take pride in their heritage. The country's ancient art and culture are some of

The New Library of Alexandria features a wall of calligraphic carvings in 120 languages, representing the world's civilizations.

human history's brightest achievements. Indeed, Egypt boasts seven World Heritage sites designated by the United Nations Organization for Education, Science and Culture (UNESCO).

Modern Egypt has much to admire as well. One of its brightest stars is the *Bibliotheca Alexandrina*, the New Library of Alexandria, in the city of Alexandria, on Egypt's Mediterranean coast. It was constructed on or near the site of the Ancient Library of Alexandria, built in the third century BCE. The original library was one of the largest and most important libraries of the ancient world. The new structure, which opened in 2002, is much more than a library. According to its statutes, it's "an international center of exchange and communication of human knowledge and a link between an East with an authentic heritage and a West with the means of scientific and technological progress."

The impressive complex includes the library itself; a documentation and research center; a library for the blind; a children's library, which hosts exhibitions of manuscripts, calligraphy, maps, and photography; a science museum, with an astronomical research unit and other places for scientific and educational programs; restoration laboratories; and an archaeological museum. This newest of Egypt's amazing achievements aspires to be, it says on its website, "The world's window on Egypt, and Egypt's window on the world."

GEOGRAPHY

The stark contrast between the fertile Nile Valley and the desert beyond is a defining feature of Egypt's geography.

1

WITHOUT THE NILE, EGYPT wouldn't be Egypt. Without this "damp little trickle of life,"—as the British writer Rudyard Kipling called it a century ago—the ancient civilization that built the great pyramids would never have blossomed here. But Egypt is more than just the river, more than the deserts, and more than the pyramids.

"The Nile, forever new and old / Among the living and the dead / Its mighty, mystic stream has rolled."
–Henry Wadsworth Longfellow
Christus, "The Golden Legend" (1872)

A *felucca*, or traditional Egyptian sailboat, glides along the Nile River at Aswan.

Egypt is largely desert land and receives very little rain. However, the Nile River flows through the country, watering a fertile green valley. North of Cairo, the river widens to form the Nile Delta as it empties into the Mediterranean Sea. Ninety-five percent of Egypt's population lives in the valley and delta of the Nile.

West of the Nile is the Libyan, or Western, Desert, with its oases; to the east lies the more mountainous and barren Arabian, or Eastern, Desert.

GEOGRAPHIC REGIONS

Egypt can be divided into four main geographic regions: the Nile Valley and Delta, the Western Desert, the Eastern Desert, and the Sinai Peninsula.

NILE VALLEY AND DELTA The Nile is the world's longest river. It flows from two lakes south of the Equator in eastern Africa northward into countries such

This photo from space shows the narrow ribbon of green that enables life in the Nile River Valley.

as Uganda and Sudan. There it leaves tropical Africa and enters desert lands, transforming them with life-giving water. On its way to the Mediterranean Sea, the river courses through Egypt, which the Greek historian Herodotus called "the gift of the Nile."

Altogether the Nile is 4,145 miles (6,671 km) long, a little longer than the Amazon River in Brazil. Some 1,000 miles (1,609 km) of the Nile run through Egypt. The Egyptians have settled the river's thin green valley that extends the length of the country. This valley is usually about 6 miles (9.7 km) wide, but is narrower in some places. In the past, the African rainy season would increase the amount of water flowing into the Nile and produce annual floods. The Aswan High Dam, completed in 1970, changed this ancient pattern.

Upon reaching the delta, the Nile splits into hundreds of branches, creating a fertile fan-shaped area that is about 100 miles (161 km) long and 155 miles (249 km) wide by the time the river finally reaches the sea. North of

Cairo, the Nile branches into the Damietta and Rosetta channels, both named after the major cities at the end of their courses. The delta contains about 60 percent of Egypt's usable land, though it also has several shallow lakes and swamps that are too salty to be used for cultivation.

THE EASTERN DESERT The Eastern Desert stretches east from the Nile River to the Red Sea coast; mountains border the Red Sea. This was once a fertile area, and it still has ancient valleys, or *wadi* (wah-DEE), that were once riverbeds. The desert also has fossilized forests, where the sand is littered with the remains of millions of ancient trees. This area is mostly uninhabited, but there are some nomadic peoples who live in the vast desert. There is more activity on the coast, which is an important center for Egypt's oil and tourism industries. Onshore and offshore drilling facilities are located there, as well as resort cities such as Hurghada.

THE WESTERN DESERT Two-thirds of Egypt's land area is covered by the Western Desert. Part of the Great Sahara, it stretches across northern Africa from the Atlantic coast all the way to the Nile Valley.

Nomads have long used camels to cross the deserts. Camels are the only domesticated animals capable of making the long, dry journey.

Most of the Western Desert consists of a sandy plateau. Close to the border is an area known as the Great Sand Sea, where the sand dunes look like waves. The wind controls the shape and movement of the dunes, and some dunes actually move a few hundred feet a year.

There are a few mountains in the Western Desert. Jabal Uweinat in the far southwest is the tallest at 6,255 feet (1,907 m). More impressive than the mountains are the great depressions that can drop several hundred feet below sea level. The largest of these is the Qattâra Depression, which at its deepest falls 436 feet (133 m) below sea level. The Qattâra starts just south of the Mediterranean coast and covers 7,000 square miles (18,130 square km).

Few spots in the world are as inhospitable as the heart of the Western Desert, where temperatures can rise as high as 120°F (49°C). Moreover, with no cloud cover to retain the heat, night temperatures tend to be very low, sometimes below freezing. Yet some species of birds, snakes, scorpions, and lizards manage to survive in the Western Desert, except in the area of shifting sand dunes.

There are six major oases in the Western Desert. The inhabitants grow palm trees and other crops to support themselves. They also work in factories, packing top-quality dates to be trucked to Cairo.

THE SINAI PENINSULA   The Sinai is a barren desert peninsula. Geographically it connects to the Asian continent. The Sinai is bordered by three bodies of water—the Gulf of Aqaba in the east, the Gulf of Suez in the west, and the Mediterranean Sea in the north. Since the completion of the Suez Canal, the Sinai has been physically cut off from the rest of Egypt.

In ancient times, the Sinai was a wild and inhospitable desert area that formed a formidable barrier between Egypt and its Middle Eastern neighbors. The ancient Egyptians did little in the region except send the occasional mining expedition in search of turquoise, copper, and other minerals. There were two major turquoise mines in the Sinai that the Egyptians exploited for thousands of years, but the mines no longer produce profitable yields.

The Sinai is flat and sandy in the north. The south is far more mountainous and boasts the highest point in Egypt—*Jabal Katrina*, or Mount Catherine, at

An oasis (the plural is oases*) is a geographical oddity. It's an isolated place of lush vegetation in a desert, fed by underground rivers or* aquifers*. (An aquifer is an underground water supply found in porous rock, sand, or gravel.) Typically, a low-lying region of the desert's surface will meet the underground water source, allowing the water to come to the surface. The high water table under the surface keeps the soil moist enough to support plant life.*

The sudden appearance of trees and grass in the middle of wide expanses of lifeless desert can be a surprising sight. Some oases are small, just large enough to support a few plants. Others are large enough to support a community. Nomads crossing deserts by camel caravan still depend on the oases for food and water, and plan their routes accordingly—just as desert travelers have done for thousands of years.

The Siwa Oasis in Egypt's Western Desert lies about 60 feet (18 m) below sea level, and is about 50 miles (80 km) long and 12 miles (20 km) wide. It has about 1,000 springs, and the water is said to be sweet and to have curative properties. This extremely remote oasis supports about 23,000 people who grow dates and olives, and make handcrafts. Almost unreachable until recently, Siwa was settled by Berber people who developed their own culture and language. Today, Siwa and some of the other Egyptian oases are "off the beaten track" tourist destinations.

8,560 feet (2,609 m). Another impressive peak in the area is Jabal Musa, or Mount Sinai, at 7,380 feet (2,249 m).

The Bedouin people have always lived in the Sinai, traditionally as nomads moving from oasis to oasis. In ancient times, the Bedouin were

Papyrus still grows along the Nile, as it has for thousands of years. The ancients used it to make a kind of paper. The English word paper derives from the Greek word for papyrus, *papuros*.

fierce warriors, and the Egyptians only ventured into the Sinai under military protection. Today many Bedouin have abandoned the nomadic way of life and instead make a living from a combination of date farming and raising livestock.

CLIMATE

Egypt has a generally hot and arid climate, but there can be a marked difference between winter and summer temperatures. Temperatures in Cairo can rise to 95°F (35°C) in summer and fall to 48°F (9°C) in winter. Farther south, the weather becomes hotter. Winters in Aswân are pleasantly warm, but summer temperatures can reach 104°F (40°C).

Alexandria in the north enjoys milder weather than the rest of the country. The highest temperature Alexandria experiences during the year does not usually rise beyond 86°F (30°C), and the cool Mediterranean breeze makes even the hottest days pleasant.

Egypt gets very little rain. Away from the influence of the Nile, Egypt quickly becomes a desert land. Cairo sees an average of five or fewer rainy days a year, and most of this rain falls between November and January. Siwa, an oasis in the middle of the Western Desert, might get rain only once or twice in a century.

FLORA

Much of Egypt's plant life is found in the Nile Valley and Delta and in the oases. The date palm, for example, is the most common indigenous tree. It has many uses, and there are at least thirty varieties of date palms in Egypt.

Papyrus, a water reed, is one of the most interesting and useful plants in Egypt. The ancient Egyptians used this plant to make sheets of paper-like material. Today papyrus grows mainly in the south of the country.

Proof of the abundance of plant life in ancient Egypt can be found in the country's fossilized forests, where the remains of trees millions of years old have turned to stone. There are no forests today in Egypt, but there are several

THE SUEZ CANAL

The Suez Canal is an artificial waterway that links the Mediterranean Sea with the Red Sea. The canal is 120 miles (193 km) long, 197 feet (60 m) wide, and 66 feet (20 m) deep— big enough to accommodate ships up to 150,000 tons in weight.

The first stretch of the Suez Canal runs from Port Said on the Mediterranean to the city of Isma'iliya on the shores of Lake Timsah. A smaller section of the canal links this lake with the Bitter Lakes. From here a third section continues to Suez and the Red Sea. The canal cuts 6,000 miles (9,656 km) off the sea journey between Europe and Asia, and three convoys make the fifteen-hour trip through the canal every day.

The Suez Canal was the brainchild of Ferdinand de Lesseps, a French diplomat posted to Egypt. In 1854 he got permission from the khedive (kai-DEV), *the Turkish governor of Egypt, to start construction. The next year, an International Technical Commission examined the possible routes, and work began in 1859. Ten years later, on November 17, 1869, a fleet of ships assembled at Port Said to make the maiden passage through the canal. They reached Suez three days later, after being entertained en route at a ball given by the khedive. Except between 1967 and 1975, when it was closed as a result of the Arab-Israeli war, the canal has been a very busy waterway and has been enlarged several times to cope with increasing traffic and bigger ships.*

common species of trees. Acacia trees grow in many parts, as do carob, eucalyptus, and sycamore trees. There are also cypress, elm, and fruit trees. Many of these trees are not indigenous but were introduced from other countries at different times in the past.

Plants in the desert areas tend to be very specialized in order to survive in the harsh environment. Examples of Egyptian desert plants are coarse alfa grass and stunted tamarisks as well as a variety of thorny shrubs and herbs.

The hoopoe is a common sight in Egypt.

FAUNA

Egypt has few large animal species. There was more wildlife in ancient times, and tomb paintings show ostriches, crocodiles, hippopotamuses, and even giraffes. Pressure from the human population has wiped them out, although there have been occasional unconfirmed reports of ostrich sightings in remote areas. Surviving species include gazelles, hyenas, and jackals, and there are also small numbers of wild boars, lynxes, and wild cats.

The camel is a well-adapted desert animal. People around the world tend to associate camels with Egypt. These "ships of the desert" were introduced to Egypt as domestic animals around the eighth century.

Egypt has more than thirty species of snakes, half of them venomous. Among the more spectacular species are the horned viper, hooded snake, and Egyptian cobra. There are also many kinds of lizards, scorpions, and insects.

There are some 200 migratory species and 150 resident species of birds. The Nile Valley is a major bird migration route between Eastern Europe and East Africa. The valley provides food for migrating birds, as they navigate along the river. Some of the most beautiful birds, such as the golden eagle— the symbol of Egypt which appears on its flag—and lammergeier, are found in the Eastern Desert and the Sinai. One of Egypt's most common birds is the hoopoe, a small, colorful ground feeder with a crest-like fan. The Nile River and the Red Sea coral gardens are home to possibly 1,000 marine species, including tiger sharks, moray eels, large perches, carps, and burls.

CAIRO

Cairo, the capital city, is known among Egyptians as "the mother of the world." Cairo sits strategically between the valley and delta of the Nile, about 100 miles from the coast. One out of eight Egyptians lives in Cairo, the political and commercial center of the country.

Cairo's population is about eleven million, making it one of the twenty largest cities in the world. The population is increasing at an alarming rate, largely due to people moving in from the countryside to seek work. This has created transportation, housing, and sanitation problems.

The Nile cuts through the city, and there are two large islands, Roda and Gezira. *Tahrir,* or "Liberation," Square is generally considered the city center. Traveling east from Tahrir Square, one passes Opera Square, the Presidential Palace, and beyond that the old city with its beautiful mosques and city gates. The western side has fewer tourist sites but is home to the University of Cairo and the middle-class neighborhoods of Muhandisin and Doqqi. From there, four-lane highways lead to the pyramids on the city's edge. The modern city center is relatively small; apart from one or two wealthy suburbs, Cairo is really a collection of villages in the middle of a vast city.

ALEXANDRIA

Alexandria is Egypt's second-largest city, with a population of more than four million people. It is situated on the Mediterranean Sea, on Egypt's north coast, and is a major international harbor. As the name suggests, it was founded by Alexander the Great and in Greek times was an important center of commerce and learning. The Lighthouse of Alexandria once stood here and was considered by some to be one of the Seven Wonders of the Ancient

The beautiful city of Alexandria reflects in the waters of the Mediterranean Sea.

World. The world's first great public library was founded here.

Today Alexandria enjoys a more cosmopolitan atmosphere than the rest of Egypt. The cooling Mediterranean breezes give it a pleasant climate, and many summer homes are built close to the beaches. The city has a good museum and a well-preserved Roman amphitheater.

In addition to the usual forms of transportation, central Alexandria is linked by a tram network. Alexandria is Egypt's chief port and the center of a major industrial region. Businesses in the area take advantage of the city's harbor facilities.

EGYPT'S OTHER CITIES

ASYUT is an important commercial center and university town in central Egypt. It has a large Christian community. Once a major resting point on the caravan route, today Asyut is a center for cotton spinning and pottery.

ASWAN Situated deep in southern Egypt, Aswan is the last major urban area before the Sudanese border. In ancient times, the pharaohs quarried some of their best granite from this area. Present-day Aswan is famous for the High Dam, and several industries are located here.

LUXOR is a resort town north of Aswan. Luxor's wealth is based on its ancient treasures—it stands on the site of ancient Thebes, the capital of Egypt for much of the pharaonic era. Luxor is linked to Cairo by good rail and road connections, and it has an international airport.

PORT SAID was founded in 1856 as a base for the construction and operation of the Suez Canal. Since then it has grown into a city of nearly half a million people. It is Egypt's second largest port and a free trade zone where many Egyptians go to buy foreign-made electronic goods.

Hot air balloons rise over the city of Luxor on the Nile River. With its wealth of ancient temples and ruins, Luxor has been called the "world's greatest open-air museum."

SUEZ AND PORT TAWFIQ guard the southern end of the canal. The ancient Egyptians built a fortress here, and the present city was founded in the fifteenth century. Although Suez was almost totally destroyed in the 1973 war, the reopening of the canal and the oil boom have seen it prosper. Today it is a thriving city of about half a million people.

INTERNET LINKS

www.bibalex.org

Bibliotheca Alexandrina (The New Library of Alexandria)

This English-language site has wonderful pictures of this magnificent new library and its museums and collections in the photo gallery.

www.ancientegypt.co.uk/geography/home.html

The British Museum

This site has interactive stories, maps, and challenges.

www.suezcanal.gov.eg/

This official site of the Suez Canal offers a wealth of information including its history and its plans for the future.

HISTORY

Engraved columns adorn the Temple of Isis on Philae Island in Lake Nasser.

2

EGYPT IS THE HOME OF ONE OF the world's first great civilizations. Around 5,000 years ago, an advanced culture developed in this land and it lasted almost 3,000 years.

People began to settle along the Nile more than 6,000 years ago. The soil in the river valley was very fertile, and hunter-gatherers gradually abandoned their old way of life to become farmers. The surrounding desert land protected the settlements in the valley from invaders, thus enabling these early inhabitants to prosper. As the population grew, the settlements merged until they formed two kingdoms: one in the valley (Upper Egypt); the other centered in the Nile Delta (Lower Egypt).

The Great Pyramids in Giza, Egypt, are the country's top tourist destination.

The word *pharaonic* means "relating to to the time of the pharaohs," the ancient Egyptian rulers. The word *pharaonism* refers to the idea that the identity of today's Egyptians, as a people, is rooted in the ancient pharaonic culture. True Egyptian identity, it suggests, predates Islam and Arab culture, and is part of a larger Mediterranean civilization.

Around 2925 BCE, a powerful king known as Menes united the two kingdoms into a single state, creating possibly the first state in human history. A stone palette dating to around that time was discovered at the end of the nineteenth century in Kom el Ahmar, an archaeological site along the Nile. The Narmer Palette depicts a king wearing the crown of Upper Egypt victorious in battle.

No one is sure who exactly Menes was; he has been linked to two names—Narmer and Aha—inscribed on the Palermo Stone, an ancient record that lists Egypt's kings from the first to the fifth dynasties. The king called Menes founded the first in a line of thirty ancient Egyptian dynasties. He established his capital at Memphis, which is very close to present-day Cairo.

The ancient Egyptians developed many inventions, such as a paper-like material called *papyrus*. They also invented *hieroglyphs*, one of the earliest forms of written language; a 365-day calendar, and the world's first national government. The Egyptians were also noted mathematicians, poets, doctors, and soldiers. Most of all, the Egyptians are remembered for their building achievements, and their magnificent temples and pyramids remain to tell the tale.

OLD KINGDOM (2575-2130 BCE)

By the end of the third dynasty, around 2575 BCE, Egypt was a firmly established nation with a strong central government. The Old Kingdom rulers also built the greatest monuments that the world had ever seen—the famous pyramids of Egypt.

The first Egyptian pyramid, the Step Pyramid at Saqqara, was a tomb for one of Egypt's greatest kings—Djoser. Redesigned three times, the Step Pyramid eventually rose nearly 200 feet (60 m) in six giant steps. The mastermind behind the Step Pyramid was Imhotep, King Djoser's chief advisor. Apart from being an architect, Imhotep was a priest, scientist, doctor, and writer. So remarkable were his achievements that later generations of Egyptians worshiped him as a god. His masterpiece, the world's oldest all-stone structure of its size, remains a tribute to his genius.

Succeeding pharaohs tried to outdo their predecessors in the size and grandeur of the pyramids that they built. Snefru, the first king of the fourth dynasty, built several pyramids, including the Bent Pyramid (named so because it angles into a gentler slope about halfway up) and the Red Pyramid (named so because of its pink limestone).

The Step Pyramid of Djoser, in the Saqqara burial region, is the oldest of Egypt's ninety-seven pyramids.

Snefru's monuments were significant achievements, but soon the next king, Khufu, built a bigger pyramid a few miles north. This is the Great Pyramid at Giza. The completed structure reached some 480 feet (146 m) in height. The Great Pyramid is the oldest and only surviving structure of the Seven Wonders of the Ancient World.

The Old Kingdom was also a time for ambitious exploration: the Egyptians traded actively with Nubia to the south (a region in today's southern Egypt and northern Sudan), sent turquoise and copper mining expeditions into the Sinai, and sailed to the Phoenician coast (today's Lebanon) to trade for cedar, olive oil, and wine.

The eighth dynasty saw the last days of the Old Kingdom; Egyptian dynastic history then entered an intermediate period. During the ninth dynasty a power struggle of sorts arose between the pharaohs and some of their high officials, and the pharaohs' pyramids declined while the tombs of local rulers became more elaborate. Widespread conflict gradually led to the formation of twin dynasties.

MIDDLE KINGDOM (1980-1630 BCE)

Without an effective central government, Egypt went through a long period of political instability before the competing dynasties were again unified, around 2060 BCE. Mentuhotep, the fourth king of the eleventh dynasty,

The Karnak temples in Thebes are the second most popular tourist site in Egypt, after the pyramids at Giza.

which had its capital at Thebes, and succeeding kings restored Egypt's power and wealth. They rebuilt the central government, sent a large army into Palestine (perhaps to protect trade links), and repaired irrigation systems. Sesostris III built a string of forts to secure Egypt's southern border. During the Middle Kingdom, Egyptian ships sailed as far as Syria, Crete, and Greece.

It was also a golden age for art. Artists produced beautiful royal sculpture, and even non-royal people had wooden models of soldiers, houses, and animals placed in their tombs. The Middle Kingdom pharaohs built pyramids almost as large as the great pyramids of the Old Kingdom.

Meanwhile, immigrants from west Asia were settling in the Nile Delta. Toward the end of the Middle Kingdom, around 1630 BCE, the immigrants grew more powerful. From among them a new line of kings arose who threatened the rule of the Egyptian pharaohs in Egypt. This immigrant dynasty was named the Hyksos dynasty, probably derived from an Egyptian term meaning "rulers of foreign lands." The Hyksos ruled a large part of Egypt from their capital at Avaris, in the Nile Delta, for nearly a century.

NEW KINGDOM (1558-1080 BCE)

The Hyksos brought new technology to Egypt, particularly in matters of warfare. The horse and chariot was introduced during this period. At the end of the seventeenth century BCE, the Egyptians ruling from Thebes began a struggle to drive out the Hyksos. This campaign peaked during the reign of Ahmose, who reclaimed land that had been under Hyksos rule. Thus began the era of the New Kingdom, when Thebes became the most important city in Egypt.

Often characterized as Egypt's Golden Age, or the Age of Empire, Egypt's

THE MYSTERIOUS LIFE AND DEATH OF KING TUT

For more than 3,000 years, the body of a little-known boy king remained untouched and undiscovered under the Egyptian sands. Most of the other pharaoh's tombs had been looted and vandalized in ancient times. In 1922, after years of searching, British archaeologist Howard Carter uncovered the mystery. He discovered King Tutankhamen's tomb in the Valley of the Kings, a burial place for pharaohs and ancient dignitaries, on the west bank of the Nile River.

The tomb contained an astonishing treasure trove of riches: gold jewelry and a solid gold death mask, statues and other works of art, thrones, beds, and the mummified body of young Tut himself. The boy became king when he was just nine years old and died at nineteen around 1324 BCE.

Throughout the twentieth century, many questions about the boy king remained unanswered. Why did he die so young? Had he been murdered? Axed in the head? Poisoned? For nearly ninety years, such theories abounded.

In 2010, new technology made possible a DNA study of the mummy. The study revealed that the king had been a frail, sickly, young man with a deformed left foot who walked with a limp—which explained the many canes found in the tomb. He had suffered from malaria, a potentially-fatal mosquito-borne disease common to tropical regions, which would have further weakened him. Scientists now believe he fell, wounding his leg, and an infection set in, which killed him.

King Tut, as he is popularly known, was a relatively unimportant pharaoh in the grand sweep of ancient Egyptian history. But today he is unquestionably Egypt's most famous king, thanks to the revelations of his long-forgotten tomb.

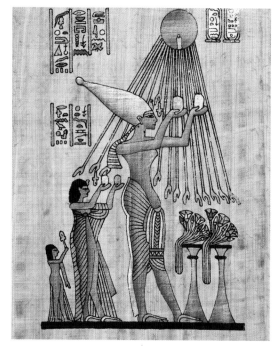

New Kingdom lasted about 500 years. Encompassing dynasties eighteen through twenty, this period of Egyptian history is considered by many scholars to be the high point of ancient Egyptian achievements in art, religion, and literature. Under a series of warrior kings, Egypt became a dominant force in the Near East, with kings from as far away as Syria paying homage to the pharaoh. Egypt also became richer than ever before, with gold, copper, ivory, and ebony pouring in from other lands.

To prevent plunderers from desecrating their treasure-filled tombs, the pharaohs of the eighteenth dynasty invented a new royal burial style. Rather than build an above-ground monument, like a pyramid, they burrowed into the earth and dug out the below-ground, hidden tombs that dot the Valley of the Kings.

Pharaoh Akhenaten (with blue headdress), his queen Nefertiti, and their daughter Meritaten (shown in sizes reflecting their importance) make a water offering to the god Aten, who is always shown as a solar disk. This painting on papyrus dates to around the fourteenth century BCE.

AMENHOTEP IV In the middle of the fourteenth century BCE, Amenhotep IV threw Egypt into turmoil by raising the status of the sun god, Aton, to that of supreme god of the universe. Amenhotep IV changed his name to Akhenaton, which meant servant of the Aton, and assumed the power of the priestly class. He also built a new capital city at Amarna.

This was a wonderful time for artists, who were allowed to explore different styles. The resulting art of Amarna thus had a more natural, less contrived appearance. However, rivalry between Akhenaton and the priests of the old, *polytheistic* (multiple gods) religion created civil unrest. Domestic problems weakened Egypt's power in the Near East and led to the loss of land in Syria. Akhenaton's religion died with him; his son and successor, the child king Tutankhamen, was forced by the priests to revive the old religion.

RAMESSES II In accomplishments, Ramesses II may be ranked as one of the most important and effective rulers of the ancient world. Truly deserving of his nickname, "the Great," Ramesses II had the longest recorded reign (sixty-seven years), fought more battles, and produced more statuary and buildings than any other ruler of ancient Egypt. He also fathered more than 100 children and lived to be more than ninety years old.

Shortly after coming to the throne, Ramesses II initiated what was to be the most-recorded military campaign in the history of the ancient Near East—the Battle of Kadesh. It was fought against the Hittites, people from a land that today encompasses parts of Turkey and Syria. Both sides claimed victory, and conflicts continued afterward. Eventually the warring nations agreed to the terms of peace. A record of the peace treaty appears on the walls of a few Egyptian temples and on Hittite clay tablets. The rest of Ramesses' reign was marked more by domestic building projects and diplomatic successes than by military activities.

The pharaoh Ramesses II stares into eternity at his temple in Luxor.

EGYPT FALLS TO FOREIGN RULE

The New Kingdom ended around 1075 BCE. Egypt was split in two parts, one ruled by pharaohs, the other by priests. The country gradually fell to invaders, such as the Assyrians and Persians, who founded their own short-lived lines of kings in Egypt. In 332 BCE, Alexander the Great swept in from Macedonia with his army and absorbed Egypt into his vast empire. He stayed in Egypt for a while and founded the city of Alexandria. After his death in 323 BCE, his general Ptolemy began a new line of rulers in Egypt.

The last of the Ptolemies, Cleopatra VII, ruled in the first century BCE. Cleopatra VII formed an alliance with Julius Caesar and then with Mark Antony, co-ruler of Rome with Octavian. Cleopatra and Mark Antony sailed to battle against Octavian at Actium, Greece, but were defeated. They fled to Alexandria, where they committed suicide the following year. Their tragic story would inspire poets, painters, writers, and musicians for centuries to come—most famously, William Shakespeare's play, *Antony and Cleopatra*, written around 1606 CE.

The only carving of Cleopatra in existence shows her with her son, on the Temple of Hathor, Dendara.

After that, Egypt came under Roman rule. Like the Greeks before them, the Romans left the Egyptians to their ancient religion. That changed with the arrival of Christianity, and from the fourth century CE, Egypt was rapidly converted to a Christian country.

ISLAMIC EGYPT

When the Roman Empire split in 395 CE, Egypt went to the Byzantine (eastern Roman) emperors. Byzantine rule continued until around 639, when Egypt fell to the Arabs. The Arabs established their capital at Fustat, which would grow into the great city of Cairo. They influenced the people of Egypt more than any of the earlier conquerors did. Most Egyptians embraced Islam, and Arabic became widely spoken.

Under the Arabs, Egypt became part of the Islamic Empire. First the Umayyad dynasty ruled the province from Damascus; then Egypt came under the jurisdiction of the Baghdad-based Abbasid dynasty.

From 868 to 969, the Turkish dynasties of Tulunid and Ikhshidid had autonomous rule over Egypt, while still acknowledging Baghdad's authority. But the two branches of Islam, the Shia and the Sunni, began a struggle for control. In 973 the Shia Muslim Fatimids established their own caliphate, which is an Islamic state led by a supreme religious and political leader called a caliph. This state was independent of the Sunni Muslim Abbasids. The Fatimids had their capital in Cairo (*Al Kahira* in Arabic, meaning "the conqueror"), which has been the capital ever since.

In the twelfth century, Crusaders from Europe invaded Egypt. The Crusaders were Christian warriors, intent on securing the Holy Lands for the Roman Catholic Church. They invaded the Middle East in various campaigns over the course of two centuries. The caliph of Syria sent the Fatimids military assistance. A Kurdish general, Salah ad Din ibn Ayyub (better known as Saladin), defeated the Crusaders. However, in 1171 Saladin overthrew the Fatimids and founded the Ayyubid dynasty. He returned Egypt to Sunni Islam and in 1187 drove the Crusaders out of Jerusalem, thus becoming a hero of the Islamic world. His descendants employed Turkish slaves—Mamluks—as bodyguards. Being very loyal, the Mamluks quickly rose to high positions in the army and government, and in 1250, loyalty aside, the Mamluks seized the sultanate. The Mamluks ruled until 1517, when they were overthrown by the Ottoman Turks.

Egypt faded from the focus of world events under Ottoman rule in the sixteenth and seventeenth centuries. Then in 1798 the country made a dramatic comeback to the world stage, when it was invaded by French forces led by Napoleon Bonaparte.

Bonaparte hoped to create a French colony and disrupt England's communications with the British Empire in India. His hopes were dashed when a British fleet led by Lord Nelson defeated the French fleet a month later. The next year Bonaparte returned to France, and in 1801 British and Ottoman forces drove the French out of Egypt.

THE MUHAMMAD ALI DYNASTY

In 1803 the British left Egypt, leaving the land to the Ottoman Turks, whose army maintained control over Egypt. However, a young Albanian officer in the army—Muhammad Ali—challenged the Ottoman Turks. In 1805, after a revolt against the Ottoman ruler, Ali became Egypt's new leader, and declared himself to be Khedive, or emperor. He reigned for forty-three years, the longest in the history of modern Egypt. He developed a centralized government system and increased contact with the West, and is called "the father of modern Egypt." He created new ministries and schools, built canals, introduced cotton to the country, and developed a textile industry. By the time of his death, Egypt had acquired an international standing.

Ali's heirs would rule Egypt until 1952. In the hands of Ali's successors, Egypt became increasingly more Westernized. Ali's fourth son, Said, ruled from 1854 to 1863. He permitted France to construct a canal across the

The Ptolemaic rulers governed Egypt for three centuries, from the new city of Alexandria. They built the Library of Alexandria, which housed the greatest works of science and the arts. Egypt's capital also became an economic hub, producing practical and luxury goods such as papyrus and perfume, and served as a port for goods moving between Africa and Europe.

On a great plateau in Giza, on the west bank of the Nile, a most unusual creature rests in the sands. It faces the rising sun and guards three large pyramids. It has stood—or actually, crouched—there for more than 4,000 years. The stone creature has the head of a man and the body of a lion. It is a mythological creature known in various cultures as a sphinx. *The lion is a common symbol of royalty, and this monument probably portrays a king. But, as was the custom, pharaohs were also deities, and the Sphinx is also a god—a sun god. (Vandals knocked off his nose many centuries ago.)*

It is enormous. In fact, it is probably the largest and oldest freestanding monument ever built—241 feet (73.5 m) long, 63 feet (19.3 m) wide, and 66.34 feet (20.22 m) high. Its head and upper body were carved from one huge rock. The colossal creature dates to the Old Kingdom period of Egyptian history, and was probably built during the reign of the Pharaoh Khafra (c. 2558–2532 BCE). But no one knows for sure when the Sphinx was built or who built it.

That's not the only riddle surrounding the Sphinx. An ancient Greek myth (dating much later, about 600 BCE) features a sphinx as a man-eating monster. The sphinx asks a riddle of all who wish to pass, and when they cannot answer it, the monster devours them. The riddle is this: "What has one voice, and is four-footed, two-footed, and three-footed?" According to the myth, many unfortunate travelers were stumped, and therefore killed. Along comes the mythical Greek king Oedipus, who answers, "Man." (Man crawls on all fours as an infant, walks on two legs at maturity, and uses a cane (three legs) in old age.) At the sound of the correct answer, the sphinx kills herself.

Folklore connects the myth with the Great Sphinx of Giza, but it probably wasn't meant to be. For one thing, the Greek sphinx is a female. Nevertheless, the "Riddle of the Sphinx" has come to be associated with the mysterious Egyptian monument.

Suez. This made Egypt strategically important to the great European powers, but it also made the country increasingly vulnerable to political events elsewhere.

Lavish spending put Egypt into debt. In 1875 its rulers sold their shares in the Suez Canal to Britain. British influence in Egypt grew so strong that they were soon interfering in Egypt's domestic issues. Anti-British uprisings led to a British military invasion. Although the British initiated some positive reforms, they were nevertheless a foreign occupying force in Egypt, and an independence movement began to develop.

Mohammad Ali (1769-1849).

THE STRUGGLE FOR INDEPENDENCE

As World War I broke out in 1914, Britain declared Egypt a protectorate and sent troops to guard the Suez Canal. This intensified anti-British sentiments in Egypt and strengthened the nationalist movement led by Saad Zaghlul. Britain granted Egypt independence in 1922, but kept the right to station troops in the country. During World War II, hundreds of thousands of British troops passed through the land.

Egypt emerged from World War II determined to rid itself of foreign influence. It devoted itself to the Arab cause and was involved in the formation of the Arab League. In 1948, when Palestine was divided into Arab and Jewish states, Egypt joined Iraq, Jordan, and Syria in the war against Israel. Egypt's defeat triggered riots in the country. In 1952 a group of army officers headed by Colonel Gamal Abdel Nasser seized power and started to tackle Egypt's serious social problems. A major reform was the Land Act, which broke up the big estates and gave land to the *fellahin*, Egypt's farm laborers.

THE SITUATION WITH ISRAEL

Egypt's relationship with Israel remained hostile long after World War II. As a leader of the Arab world, Egypt wished to see the land of Israel returned to the Palestinians. In 1967 Egypt entered a military alliance with Syria and Jordan and closed the Gulf of Aqaba to Israeli shipping. The Israelis, seeing the blockade as an act of war, launched an attack on Egypt, destroying most of the Egyptian air force on the ground. Israel defeated Egypt in the Six-Day War, taking control of the Sinai and the Gaza Strip from Egypt, the West Bank and East Jerusalem from Jordan, and the Golan Heights from Syria.

The Soviet Union gave military equipment worth millions of dollars to rebuild the Egyptian army. After several border incidents threatened to restart the war, the United States and the United Nations arranged a ceasefire.

On October 6, 1973, in an attempt to regain land captured by Israel in the 1967 Six-Day War, Egyptian and Syrian forces attacked Israel. This attack, backed by many other Arab nations as well as by the Soviet Union, would become known as the "Yom Kippur War," because it began on the Day of Atonement (Yom Kippur), the holiest day in the Jewish calendar. (The war is also called "The Ramadan War," because it took place during the Muslim holy

Egyptian President Anwar Sadat, left, U.S. President Jimmy Carter, center, and Israeli Prime Minister Menachem Begin clasp hands after signing a historic peace treaty between Egypt and Israel on March 26, 1979, at the White House.

month of Ramadan; or simply, "The October War.") Egyptian troops stormed the fortifications along the Suez Canal and overran the Sinai. Taken by surprise, at first the Israelis were overwhelmed. Within days, however, Israel, backed by the United States, counterattacked and pushed out the invaders. A ceasefire brought the hostilities to an end on October 25.

Although the attack was ultimately unsuccessful, Egyptians gained a renewed confidence in their military capability and felt strong enough to seek peace. In 1978, Egypt and Israel signed the Camp David Accords, an agreement which required Israel to return the rest of the Sinai to Egypt (having returned part of it in 1975). Then in 1979, the two countries concluded a peace treaty, the first between Israel and an Arab nation. This greatly angered the Arab world, and Egypt was dismissed from the Arab League.

Over the years, Egypt's relations with the Arab world improved and its membership in the Arab League was reinstated in 1989. Egypt continued to play a crucial role in Middle Eastern conflicts. When Iraq was primed to invade neighboring Kuwait in 1990, Egypt initiated negotiations between those two countries. The negotiations failed, and Iraq invaded its neighbor, which led to the Persian Gulf War in 1991. Egypt then sent troops to support a massive coalition to free Kuwait from Iraqi occupation. In 1993 Egypt facilitated a peace accord between Israel and the Palestine Liberation Organization.

THE PRESIDENTIAL ERA

Egypt was a constitutional monarchy until 1952, when a group of army officers seized control of the government. They considered the regime of King Farouk I to be corrupt and pro-British. This event, which became known as the Egyptian Revolution of 1952, forced King Farouk into exile. Egypt became a republic headed by its first president, the former Army General Muhammad Naguib.

In 1956, Gamal Abdel Nasser, who took part in the overthrow of King Farouk, became Egypt's second president. He worked to modernize Egypt and rid it of all former colonial influence and negotiated a withdrawal of British troops. He seized control of the Suez Canal from Britain and France,

and constructed the Aswan High Dam on the Nile River. Under his direction, the government took over much of Egypt's industry and many new factories were built. Nasser emphasized Arab dignity, pride, and power, and became an enormously popular public figure both at home and throughout the Arab Middle East. In 1967, however, Egypt suffered a disastrous military defeat in the Six-Day War against Israel, which was a blow to Nasser's reputation. Nevertheless, he remained president of Egypt until he died in 1970. He is still much revered to this day.

Egypt's next president, Anwar el-Sadat, began serious peace talks with Israel. In 1979, he and Israeli Prime Minister Menachim Begin shared the Nobel Peace Prize for their work. The following year, their two nations signed a peace treaty. It was the first—and remains the only—such treaty between Israel and an Arab country. Not everyone in Egypt was happy with the peace treaty, however, and Sadat's popularity fell at home. In 1981, extremists assassinated the president at a military parade in Cairo.

Hosni Mubarak, Sadat's successor, was Egypt's president for nearly 30 years. During his time in office, Egypt enjoyed years of economic growth and stability. However, for most of that time, the president kept the country under emergency law. That gave the government more power and greatly restricted individual freedoms.

THE 'ARAB SPRING'

In 2011, Mubarak was forced from power following a wave of mass protests. The demonstrations were part of a series of uprisings throughout the Arab world that became known as the "Arab Spring." People took the streets to protest authoritarian rulers. They demanded democratic governments and more individual rights and freedoms. The uprisings in Egypt focused on similar demands, but were met with harsh military actions, violence, and bloodshed. Some 850 people died and thousands were injured. Those eighteen days of protests came to be called the January 25 Revolution.

Mubarak was eventually charged with corruption and involvement in the deaths of the anti-government protesters. Egypt itself, along with other Arab nations—such as Libya and Tunisia—entered a period of transformation. Hopes were high for the first free presidential election, which was won in 2012 by Mohamed Morsi of the Muslim Brotherhood, a Sunni Islamist political party. But the election process highlighted the deep disagreement among Egyptians over the role of Islam in politics and society. Morsi favored Islamist rule, but his opponents believed the government should be more secular, or without religious influence. After Morsi had served as president for only one year, Egypt's military forced him out of office in July 2013. A transitional government was put in place.

On January 25, 2012, protesters in Cairo mark the first anniversary of the 2011 uprising.

INTERNET LINKS

www.sis.gov.eg (choose English)

Egypt State Information Service

This official Egyptian government site is full of news, information, and photos on a wide range of topics.

www.bbc.co.uk/history/ancient/egyptians

www.history.com/topics/ancient-history/ancient-egypt

These are two wonderful interactive sites about Egypt's ancient history.

www.smithsonianmag.com/history/uncovering-secrets-of-the-sphinx-5053442

This site features an in-depth story with a video and a photo gallery.

GOVERNMENT

The colors of the Egyptian flag represent oppression (black), which was overcome through bloody struggle (red), to be replaced by a bright future (white). The gold Eagle of Saladin in the center is the symbol of Egypt.

3

W ITH POLITICAL CHANGE TAKING place so rapidly over the last few years, the Egyptian government has been in a period of transformation. The president's role, and the structure of the government itself, may be subject to change amid the current upheaval.

In January 2014, Egyptians approved a new constitution, though violence marred the two days of voting. Under the new constitution,

- the president may serve two four-year terms. Such an arrangement would prevent prolonged regimes, such as Mubarak's. Previously, the president could serve for six years and be re-elected an unlimited number of times.
- Islam remains the state religion, but freedom of religion provides protection to minorities,
- men and women are equal under the law, and
- political parties may not be formed based on religion, race, gender, or geography.

EXECUTIVE BRANCH

Since the overthrow of the monarchy, Egypt has had three branches of government: the executive branch, the legislature, and the judicial branch. The executive branch is headed by the president. He or she must be at least forty years old, must be Egyptian, and born of Egyptian

"Egyptians are like camels: they can put up with beatings, humiliation and starvation for a long time but when they rebel they do so suddenly and with a force that is impossible to control."
–Alaa Al Aswany, from *On the State of Egypt: A Novelist's Provocative Reflections* (2011)

parents. The president is the head of the country and exercises the powers spelled out in the constitution. These powers include choosing the prime minister, who acts as the president's deputy and puts his policies into action. The president also chooses the members of the cabinet, called the Council of Ministers. And he or she decides other important matters that affect Egypt and its relationship with other countries.

LEGISLATURE (PARLIAMENT)

From 1980 until 2011, the legislature, or parliament, was a bicameral, or two-house governmental body. But following the revolution in 2011, the parliament was dissolved and the constitution scrapped. The 264-member upper house, the Shura Council, was abolished. The 2014 constitution calls for a unicameral, or one-house, legislature. This is the House of Representatives, or People's Assembly. This law-making body is made up of at least 450

Supporters of Egypt's ousted president Mohammed Morsi protest his trial in front of the Supreme Constitutional Court on Nov. 4, 2013. He was charged with incitement to violence and murder.

members who serve five-year terms. Most are elected by popular vote and up to ten are appointed by the president. This branch of government drafts laws and amendments to the constitution, approves international agreements and treaties, and oversees the work of the executive branch.

JUDICIARY BRANCH

The judicial branch is the court system. There are three levels of courts, each overseeing various levels of disputes, both civil and criminal. These courts do not use a jury system. In addition, there is the Supreme Constitutional Court, the highest court in the republic. It reviews the constitutionality of the rulings of the lower courts and settles disputes between them. At a lower level, there are special courts for economic, military, family, labor, security, and other matters. Family courts, in particular, administer Islamic Shari'a law, though Islamic law is considered the basis of all national law.

Egyptian women vote at a polling station in Shubrah El-Kheima, on the outskirts of Cairo. They are voting in the landmark presidential runoff on June 16, 2012. Mohammad Morsi would win this election, but be forced from office after only one year.

GOVERNORATES

At the regional level, Egypt is divided into twenty-six administrative units called governorates. They are something like states or counties. Each governorate has a governor appointed by the president. The governor works with an elected council to manage matters such as the building of a new hospital or school. Each governorate consists of smaller administrative units, such as districts and villages. These are managed by mayors with their own elected councils.

The Mugamma, a government office building in Cairo

FOREIGN POLICY

Egypt has been a crossroads of commerce and culture for thousands of years. That position makes it a nation of major political importance in the Arab world, the Middle East, Africa, and the world. Egypt's foreign policy is based on its status as a non-aligned nation. That means it is not formally allied with or against any powerful nation or group of nations.

Since the establishment of the Arab League in 1945, Egypt has placed Arab issues among its main interests. Egypt's role in the 1948 Arab-Israeli war demonstrated Egypt's sense of belonging in the Arab world. However, Egypt's commitment to the Israeli peace process has strained its relations with the Arab states. Therefore, Egypt has tried to strike a fragile balance in its Middle Eastern policy decisions—working to restore Arab relations on the one hand and pushing forward with the Israeli peace process on the other. It has also played a role in trying to resolve the Israeli-Palestinian conflict.

Egypt has also supported the struggle for independence in other Arab countries. However, it maintains a policy of non-intervention in the affairs of its neighbors. The relationship between Egypt and the United States has been challenged by the recent rapid changes in Egyptian politics. The United States officially supports Egypt's transition to democracy, and desires a strong, secure friend in the Arab world. However, U.S. officials disagree on how to respond to the recent events. Many Americans are concerned about the Egyptian military crackdown on government protesters. In Egypt, on the other hand, a popular streak of anti-Americanism further complicates the relations between the two nations.

On Nov. 16, 2012, protesters in Cairo demonstrated against a recent Israeli invasion of Gaza. The Arabic words on the American flag say, "Death to Israel and death to America."

INTERNET LINKS

www.cia.gov/library/publications/the-world-factbook/geos/eg.html

The CIA World Factbook has up-to-date facts and statistics.

www.cia.gov/library/publications/the-world-factbook/geos/eg.html

In the CIA World Factbook, click on "World Leaders" in the left margin for a list of Egypt's government officials.

www.sis.gov.eg (choose English)

Egypt State Information Service

An excellent site full of news, information, and photos on a wide range of Egyptian topics.

ECONOMY

Sweet dates hang in bunches from a date palm. The fruit is an important commodity in Egypt's economy.

4

WITH THE SECOND LARGEST economy in the Arab world, Egypt relies on four main sources of income: oil and petrochemical exports, Suez Canal tolls, tourism receipts, and money sent home to Egypt by Egyptians working abroad.

In recent years, however, political instability has greatly hurt the country's economy—particularly the critically important tourism industry. During times of revolution and transition, countries typically

A big red oil tanker passes through the Suez Canal. The trip takes about fifteen hours but saves up to two months of time the tanker would have spent going the long way around Africa.

"Stop all kinds of sit-ins, protests, and strikes. Let us start building the nation. ... No voice must be louder than the voice of construction and development."
– Ibrahim Mehlib, Prime Minister of Egypt, March 1, 2014.
Mehlib called on Egyptians to give the nation a chance to rebuild after three years of political turmoil had devastated the economy.

face economic difficulties, and Egypt has been going through this phase. As Egyptians struggle to create a stable new government, the future of the nation's financial business also hangs in the balance.

A SCARCITY OF LAND FOR FARMING

Although other sectors have overtaken it as a money earner, agriculture remains one of the mainstays of the Egyptian economy. It is the largest employer, providing jobs to about a third of the population. Apart from direct employment in agriculture, agriculture-based industries and services are also very important to Egypt's economic prospects.

Egypt has approximately 22,000 square miles (57,000 square km) of land under cultivation. Given the shortage of arable land, the Egyptian government has paid special attention to reclaiming desert land, as it did through the building of the Aswan High Dam in the 1950s. Reclamation

Flowers bloom along the banks of Lake Nasser, an artificial lake created by the construction of the Aswan High Dam.

projects have helped to create new agricultural land, but housing construction also competes for more land. In addition, poor drainage has raised salinity (salt) levels in some areas, hindering attempts to cultivate crops as far as was thought possible with land reclamation projects.

Because Egypt has virtually no rain, all crops depend on irrigation. Egypt has been drawing water from the Nile since pharaonic times. Since the construction of the Aswan High Dam, Lake Nasser has been storing excess floodwater, forming the world's largest human-made lake in the process. This floodwater provides for the country's water needs all year.

Egyptian cotton is considered among the finest in the world because its extra long fibers produce very smooth fabric.

IMPORTANT CROPS

Cotton, rice, corn, and sorghum are Egypt's main summer crops, while wheat, vegetables, and Egyptian clover are the main winter crops. Egypt is self-sufficient in fruit and vegetables, but overall food production has lagged behind the needs of a rapidly growing population. Today, Egypt imports about 40 percent of its food.

Cotton is the main cash crop, accounting for nearly one-fifth of Egypt's export earnings and providing the base for the domestic spinning and weaving industry.

Egyptians eat a great deal of bread, and the country does not produce sufficient wheat for its needs. It is the world's largest wheat importer, bringing in about 11 million tons (10 million tonnes) a year, around half its annual consumption.

The 1952 land reforms divided the big farms of rich landowners into small units and gave them to the *fellahin*, or peasants. Farmers sell cotton, sugarcane, and half their rice harvest to the government. However, as the fellahin's land is often too small to introduce modern farming methods, they still rely heavily on manual labor.

MANUFACTURING

During the mid-1990s, the government launched a privatization program to transfer the ownership and operation of factories from the public sector to the private. Most factories at the time were still owned or supervised by the government. Since the revolution, the public sector had to lead the country in the push for industrialization.

Privatization measures have managed to raise the productivity of factories, which are beginning to see profits after years of losses. However, the government still holds major factories and companies, such as car assembly lines and iron and steel production plants.

Manufacturing accounts for 25 percent of Egypt's production. In the past decade, many new industries have been introduced in the country and existing ones improved. Ceramics, plastics, petrochemicals, iron, steel, aluminum, cement, paper, fertilizer, textiles and fabrics, clothes, leather goods, cars, electronics, furniture, and processed foods are just some products bearing the "Made in Egypt" label. Computer software is the newest addition to Egyptian manufacturing. While agriculture is no longer the backbone of the Egyptian economy, manufacturing industries that depend mainly on agricultural products are still important.

The government is also trying to develop industry in the new cities outside the traditional population centers of Cairo and Alexandria. The government has built hundreds of new factories in these new cities and is offering investment incentives and improving infrastructure to attract investors and workers.

INTERNATIONAL TRADE

From the 1950s to the end of the 1980s, most of Egypt's manufacturing exports went to the Soviet Union and Eastern Europe. Today, the United

States and Western Europe form the main export market for Egyptian manufactured goods.

With a growing export market, Egypt has had to work hard to bring its products up to international standards. Partnership agreements with the European Union and the United States and new investment laws are boosting the quantity and quality of Egyptian manufacturing.

Despite the growing number of factories and the rising standard of Egyptian products, Egypt still has to import many items, such as food, machinery, chemicals, wood, paper, and metal products. In fact, Egypt buys more than it can sell each year. Egypt imports mainly from the European Union and the United States, as well as from other Middle Eastern countries and some Asian nations.

OIL AND GAS

The history of oil in Egypt dates to 1886 when it was first discovered in the Eastern Desert. However, the first successful oil drilling didn't begin until 1911. Egypt pioneered oil refining in the Middle East in 1913. Today, oil generates about 40 percent of Egypt's export revenue. The oil industry is largely controlled by the Egyptian General Petroleum Corporation, a state-owned organization. It works with the private sector in the exploration, processing, and distribution of oil and oil products.

Egypt's oil is found mainly in the Gulf of Suez, the Western and Eastern deserts, and the Sinai desert. The Gulf of Suez produces almost 50 percent of the nation's oil. The gulf's oil comes from both offshore fields, such as Ramadan and October, and onshore fields (on the eastern bank), such as Ras Gharib and Karim. Today, Egypt produces around 262.8 million barrels of oil per year, using the bulk of it for domestic needs. It exports the surplus, around 31 million barrels, mainly to Europe and North America.

Natural gas was first discovered in Egypt in 1967. Further finds were made in the 1980s in the Nile Delta and the Western Desert, but the gas industry still has great potential for growth. About 60 percent of the country's gas is used to generate power; the rest goes mainly to industrial use.

A network of pipelines transports crude oil and natural gas from the fields to the refineries to domestic consumers or to pipelines connecting Egypt to its export markets.

TOURISM

Egypt was one of the earliest nations to develop a booming tourist trade—during the days of steamship travel, passengers sailing through the Suez Canal often made a detour to visit the pyramids.

Today, tourism is Egypt's second most important foreign revenue earner, after oil. The modern tourist industry is served by a range of hotels of different standards and by airlines. Egypt Air and internal carriers transport passengers quickly between Cairo and other world capitals and between

Camels are sometimes adorned with vibrant colors that contrast with monochromatic desert landscapes. Here, tourists ride a camel along a beach in Egypt.

major cities in Egypt. Within a city, fleets of comfortable buses transport visitors from one site to the next.

Tourism is the ideal industry for Egypt; it employs many people and earns vital foreign exchange. Egypt's top tourist destinations are Cairo, where most visitors take excursions to the pyramids and visit the National Museum's Tutankhamen collection; and Luxor, where ancient temple ruins are the main attraction. The Sinai is also a popular area, where people enjoy snorkeling and diving or climbing Mount Sinai.

In recent years, however, Egypt's tourist industry has suffered from instability in the region. Throughout the 1990s and 2000s, there were multiple terrorist attacks aimed at tourists, with some fatal results. This terrorist activity, as well as the wars in Iraq, caused the Egyptian economy a serious loss of tourism revenue and made life harder for the many people who had come to depend on the trade. For example, Egypt suffered an 80 percent decline of tourist arrivals in February 2011. The ongoing uprisings and governmental changes have only added to the problem, as some people perceive Egypt to be a dangerous place to visit.

INTERNET LINKS

www.touregypt.net

Tour Egypt

Tour Egypt is an American tourism company, but this site has plenty of photos and information even for the non-traveler.

http://en.egypt.travel/

Egypt's official tourism website offers beautiful photos of many regions in the country.

www.sis.gov.eg/En/

State Information Service of Egypt (click on "Economy")

This offers an excellent overview of Egypt's economy during hard times.

ENVIRONMENT

There's more to Egypt than sand. The Jackson Reef in the Red Sea off Sharm el Sheikh is rich with corals and colorful sea creatures.

5

THE CONCEPT OF ENVIRONMENTAL protection may have been born in ancient Egypt. The religious beliefs of ancient Egyptians showed a respect for nature. An Egyptian religious text indicates that a person seeking forgiveness from the gods had to declare in front of a priest not only that he or she had never killed or stolen, but also that he or she had never altered the water of the Nile River.

Even today, it is widely believed in Egyptian cultural tradition that the earth and everything on it, such as water and air, are God's gifts to the human race that we are to preserve in gratitude.

However, the current condition of the natural environment in Egypt does not reflect this belief. Conservation in a densely populated country with sandy desert covering most of the land is extremely challenging. Compared to land that is newly settled, land that has been inhabited for a long time tends to be more susceptible to damage by human activity. Many parts of Egypt, especially along the Nile, have been continuously inhabited by people for more than seven thousand years. It is thus reasonable to expect environmental problems in the major cities, which have a long history of human settlement.

Nonetheless, the government and nongovernmental organizations (NGOs) are making some effort to address the country's environmental problems, with valid urgency. Prolonged environmental damage has

Egyptians get 97 percent of their water from the Nile. Much of this water is polluted. More than 350 factories located in the Nile Delta discharge untreated industrial wastes directly into the river and also into the Mediterranean Sea.

resulted in the destruction of wildlife, poor health, and the accelerated deterioration of ancient monuments, the nation's pride and heritage. These problems have become a fact of life in Egypt's crowded cities and are likely to get worse unless measures are taken to raise awareness, change settlement patterns, reduce pollution, and improve systems of garbage disposal, among other things. Financial aid from nations such as the United States is also helping Egypt achieve its environmental goals.

Even antiquity can't escape modernity. Fast food trash litters the foot of the Pyramid of Khufu in Giza.

POLLUTION

In a large city such as Cairo there are many sources of pollution: domestic waste generated by almost eighteen million people living and working in the capital; exhaust fumes from the more than two million cars traveling the streets daily; and effluents (liquid waste) released by factories into the air and waterways. It has been estimated that more than 230 billion gallons (around 870 billion liters) of industrial pollutants enter the waters of the Nile every year, the equivalent of more than 630 million gallons (around 2.4 billion liters) on average per day.

As the established cities get more and more crowded, green spaces shrink, exacerbating the air pollution problem. In Cairo, especially, this has reduced the purifying effect of the trees on the air that the inhabitants breathe every day. Air pollutants expose people to the risk of illness. More lethal than sand blown from the open desert are metal compounds suspended in the air. The air in Cairo has among the highest levels of lead particles in the world.

The treatment and disposal of solid waste in Egypt is formally carried out by the public sector. But private companies are sometimes hired to collect refuse in certain areas, such as hotels and airports, while foreign companies manage municipal solid waste in Cairo, Alexandria, and Giza. Most of Egypt's garbage is incinerated at open dump sites, which adds to air pollution. To alleviate the problem of disposal, plants are being built to recycle refuse or convert organic waste to fertilizer.

ERODING HISTORY

Another serious consequence of air pollution in Egypt is its effect on the country's ancient monuments. Perhaps the most famous proof of the effects of pollution on Egypt's pharaonic treasures is the Sphinx at Giza, whose face has been scoured and scarred by sand and other particles in the air. In the 1980s, in a bid to rescue one of the most precious symbols of the nation's history, the government initiated a ten-year restoration project involving local and international architects and archaeologists. Repair work continues as the monument grows older and less resistant to archaeological pollution.

Huge, strange chalk formations in the White Desert, one of Egypt's national parks, formed from the scouring effects of sandstorms on rocks.

A drive in the deserts of Egypt runs through awesome landscapes with curious wild-life; a dive in the Red Sea reveals picture-perfect scenes of colorful coral reefs, with equally colorful creatures such as clown fish swimming among anemone.

Egypt's wildlife is as precious a treasure as the nation's ancient monuments. Unfortunately, Egypt's plants and animals have fallen victim to pollution as have the pharaonic ruins. The UNEP World Conservation Monitoring Center has classified as threatened fifteen species of mammals, eleven bird species, six species of reptiles, and around eighty plant species in Egypt.

Another threat to Egyptian wildlife is the international black market in endangered species. Egypt has long been a transit point for the illegal wildlife trade in Africa and Asia. Trade in endangered flora and fauna is officially banned in Egypt, but enforcement of the law is difficult, given a lack of financial resources and public awareness.

A member of the Convention on International Trade in Endangered Species of Wild Flora and Fauna (CITES) since 1978, Egypt has recently stepped up its efforts to comply more actively with the convention, which requires member nations to protect their own endangered species both within and beyond their borders.

The critically endangered Egyptian tortoise is one of the world's smallest tortoises. This desert animal is virtually or nearly gone from Egypt, and populations in neighboring Libya are threatened. Illegal collecting for sale in the pet trade as well as habitat destruction have brought the species close to extinction.

ENVIRONMENTAL PROJECTS

The Egyptian government's most significant environmental projects to date include the establishment of seventy-six monitoring stations to measure air pollution, public environmental education and training campaigns, and the establishment of twenty-one nature reserves.

Egypt's protected areas occupy 8.5 percent of the nation's total land area and represent a variety of ecosystems. More sites will eventually receive protected status.

Two famous nature reserves in Egypt are the Ras Muhammad National Park at the tip of the Sinai and the Saint Catherine Protectorate in the central-southern Sinai. The 185-square mile (around 480-square km) Ras Muhammad National Park includes the Tiran and Sanafir islands. It is a haven for rare corals and numerous fish and birds. The 2,220-square mile (5,750-square km) Saint Catherine Protectorate is home to high-altitude mammals such as foxes, hyenas, wildcats, and wolves, reptiles such as snakes and geckos, and many kinds of insects.

Lake Qarun in Al Fayyum is an important wetland area populated by a wide variety of fish and birds such as ducks, eagles, flamingos, and swans. Lake Qarun is also special for its fossils, some dating back to over thirty million years ago.

In 2002 Egypt hosted the first international conference on Protected Areas and Sustainable Development. Participants came from all over the world to attend the forum, held at Sharm El-Sheikh. More than 200 studies were recorded, adding to the world's knowledge of protected areas, ecotourism, and biodiversity.

INTERNET LINKS

www.eeaa.gov.eg

Ministry of State for Environmental Affairs

The government site gives up-to-date information and news.

www.eoearth.org

Encyclopedia of Earth Enter "Egypt" into Search box.

Several excellent pages offer a topical overview of Egypt, including environmental issues. The site has great photos and maps.

EGYPTIANS

A woman proudly holds up her baby in a Nubian village near Aswan, in southern Egypt.

6

A ROUND 99 PERCENT OF EGYPT'S 85,294,000 people are ethnic Egyptians who identify as Arabs. They speak Arabic, the nation's official language, and 90 percent of them are Muslim, mostly Sunni. About 9 percent are Copts, or Coptic Christians. They are descendants of the ethnic Egyptians who never switched from Christianity to Islam many centuries ago. The Copts are the largest religious minority in Egypt, and the largest Christian community in the Middle East.

Small minority groups of people make up the remainder of the population. They are the ethnic Nubians, Berbers, Bedouins, Beja, and Dom. The Nubians are non-Arab Muslims who inhabit the region of southern Egypt and northern Sudan called Nubia. The Berbers are descendants of the pre-Arab peoples of northern Africa, who live primarily in mountain or desert regions. Most are farmers, but some are nomads. The Bedouins are Arabic-speaking nomadic peoples of the Middle Eastern deserts. Most are animal herders. The Beja people are an ethnic group mostly inhabiting Sudan. Finally, the Dom are an ethnic group distantly related to the Romani people of Eastern Europe, commonly called Gypsies. The Dom are also often called Gypsies and are almost universally discriminated against throughout the Middle East. However, one of the

"Beam of light, sun and moon. Shining beast, man and woman. I am passing through. Come outside among the people. I am light. Gaze on me. Moon in darkness, sun in morning. Light is what I will on Earth, along the Nile, among the people."
–from The Egyptian Book of the Dead (Normandi Ellis translation)

classic dances associated with this part of the world, the belly dance, arose from Dom culture.

Fellahin, or rural peasants, are the farmers of the Nile Valley and Delta. The name *fellahin* (or fellaheen) comes from the Arabic word *felaha* (feh-LAH-ha), meaning "to labor or till the earth."

BEDOUINS

The Bedouins are the most distinct tribal community in Egypt. They lived traditionally in the Western and Sinai deserts as nomads, moving their camel herds and flocks of sheep from oasis to oasis. Many Bedouins have now settled in towns and villages, although they still have a reputation for being independent and hospitable.

Camels are an important part of Bedouin life. Camels are useful as a mode of transportation and a source of food and materials: they can be milked, and

A Bedouin man bakes bread on an outdoor stove.

their hair made into tents, carpets, and clothes. Bedouin cuisine has been influenced by the limitations of desert life, and lamb and rice form a large part of their diet. Meals are generally eaten in silence, the men dining in a separate tent from the women.

Bedouins may weave rugs or make handicrafts for sale to supplement the family income. Bedouin rugs are woven on small looms and vary between tribes in style and color. Bedouin jewelry is often large and heavy, made from silver or base metal. Finger rings, earrings, and necklaces are favorites.

Over the centuries, Bedouins have become a hardy people, well-adapted to their environment. In the twentieth century, however, wars in the Sinai drove many Bedouins to the cities. The Egyptian government is encouraging Bedouins to settle, providing medical services and schools. Some Bedouins have become date farmers; some work on construction projects or in oil fields. Paid employment has changed the way Bedouins live, and cars and trucks are now common features of life in the villages.

NUBIANS

Nubians are people of African descent living in southern Egypt and northern Sudan. They tend to be tall, thin, and dark-skinned, and many Nubian women tattoo decorative patterns on their lips, hands, and feet. There are some 300,000 Nubians. They are mostly Muslim and speak Arabic as well as Nubian.

Traditional Nubian homes are made of clay and straw bricks baked hard in the sun. Both the inside and outside are usually decorated with finger-painted murals of trees and boats.

The construction of the Aswan High Dam in the 1960s flooded the Nubians' ancestral homeland along the Nile Valley in southern Egypt, and they had to resettle in new areas north of Aswan. Another consequence of the dam was the destruction of ancient Nubian treasures, part of the heritage of today's Nubian people.

The traditional Nubian economy is based on growing date palms, which provide not only food but also timber and rope. Many Nubians look for work in Egypt's cities. However, family ties remain strong, and they usually return to their home village when they have earned enough money in the city.

A Nubian man sails a felucca over the Nile in Aswan. Felucca sailboats today are much like the ones used thousands of years ago.

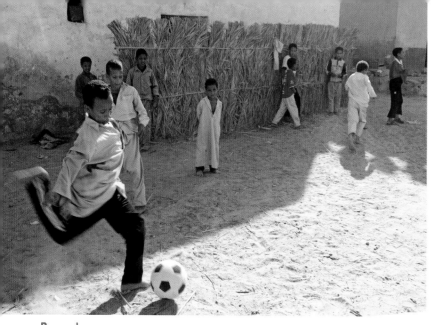

Boys play soccer in the Siwa Oasis in the Western Desert.

Like Bedouins, Nubians are known for their hospitality, which tourists can get a taste of during guided tours into Nubian villages.

PEOPLE OF THE OASES

Egyptians who live in the oases are originally of Amazigh, or Berber descent, with many later influences. Many who live in the Kharijah oasis, on the great caravan route, have dark skin, owing to their African ancestry. Whatever their ethnic mix, however, the oasis dwellers tend to see themselves as culturally different from Egyptians who live along the Nile.

The oases are blue-and-green havens in the vast desert. They are known for their natural springs, date palms and other fruit trees, and ancient ruins. The pace of change in the oases is somewhat slower than it is along the Nile, although paved roads are gradually exposing some oasis communities to modern influences such as tourism. Oases in the Western Desert include Dakhla, Farâfra, Khârga, and Siwa.

In the remote Siwa oasis, there are significant differences in customs, clothing, and language. Siwa has a population of some twenty-three thousand, and the people are a mixture of Amazigh, Bedouin, and Sudanese. Siwa women lead very restricted lives. They generally cover themselves from head to foot with a square gray woolen cloth when they are outside the home, if they are allowed to leave at all.

PEOPLE OF THE EASTERN DESERT

Two peoples, the Ababdah and the Bisharin, survive in the harsh natural environment of the Eastern Desert. These two groups belong to a larger group of people known as the Beja, who live between the Nile Valley and the Red Sea, as far south as Ethiopia.

The Ababdah live in the area immediately south of Aswan, while the Bisharin occupy the southwestern corner of Egypt, extending into the Sudan. Both groups speak a language called *To Bedawi* (TOW BAY-dah-wee), although most Ababdah and some Bisharin men also know Arabic.

The Ababdah and the Bisharin tend to be small and muscular in build and have a dark complexion. The women wear gold or silver jewelry and wrap themselves in colorful cloth. The men hang charms around their necks and wear daggers attached by leather straps to their arms.

Some members of both groups still live their traditional nomadic life in the inner desert; they call themselves the Mountain People. They take shelter from the elements in small cocoon-shaped dwellings made from tree branches and covered with rugs. These dwellings can be quickly packed and carried to a new spot whenever the group moves in search of food and water.

Few people anywhere else on the planet live in as much isolation from the rest of the world as do the Mountain People. The only outside contact they have is with former nomads who have settled in communities on the edge of the Eastern Desert. The Mountain People trade with these settlers, bringing their animals to the markets and exchanging them for sugar, coffee, flour, gold, and silver.

POPULATION GROWTH

Already the most populous country of the Middle East and the third most populous on the African continent (after Nigeria and Ethiopia), Egypt is still seeing very rapid population growth—some one million people are added to the population every year. This puts a tremendous strain on Egypt's limited resources. The United Nations projects the Egyptian population to exceed 100 million by 2030.

Although Egypt's sheer size would be sufficient to support such a population, only a fraction of the country is habitable. As urban areas on the coasts and along the Nile become more and more overcrowded, more

In Egypt's cosmopolitan urban centers, such as Cairo and Alexandria, many professional people, both men and women, wear Western-style clothing.

In the villages and rural areas, the most common dress for men is the galabia *(GEH-lah-bia)*, which resembles an ankle-length nightshirt. It has long, loose sleeves and a round neck. The winter galabia is made from flannel or heavy cotton; the summer version is lighter. Galabia generally come in dull colors. The galabia, while very much an Egyptian dress, is generally worn by other people in the Middle East as well, although in modified designs.

Underneath the galabia, Egyptian men wear cotton shirts and shorts. They may take off the galabia when working outdoors. Some men, particularly the older ones, also wear a woolen skull cap.

Egyptian women traditionally wear a long black robe similar to a galabia, called an abaya. They also wear a head covering called a hijab, *and* sometimes a face veil. Unlike some Muslim countries, Egypt has no strict laws regulating women's dress, but Islamic tradition dictates that women must dress modestly in public. Many Muslim women will cover their head and chest with the hijab, and keep their arms and legs completely covered as well. Some very conservative women will wear a garment called a burka, *which cloaks their entire body from head to toe. Some burkas leave an opening for the eyes, while others cover the eyes with mesh.*

fertile land is covered up with new buildings. As the amount of arable land for farming shrinks, and the population grows, how will Egypt feed its people?

Housing, medical systems, education, and transportation in the cities are also struggling to meet rising demands. Meanwhile, the lack of job opportunities in Egypt drives many skilled workers abroad.

Many poor people live in overcrowded urban areas, such as this neighborhood in Cairo.

INTERNET LINKS

www.sis.gov.eg/En/

State Information Service "Your Gateway to Egypt" (click on "Society")

Find a wide variety of topics about Egyptians and their communities.

www.touregypt.net/epeople.htm

TourEgypt.net

Use this link as a portal to the archives of *Tour Egypt Monthly*, an online magazine with some very interesting essays about the Egyptian people.

LIFESTYLE

A man in Aswan sells herbs, spices, and gifts at an outdoor market.

EGYPTIANS IN THE CITIES HAVE vastly different lifestyles from those in the countryside. Villagers still tend to live in close, change-resistant communities. Rural life is dominated by the daily routine of tending the crops and livestock. The greatest change to the lifestyle of rural Egyptians has been the migration of an increasing number of young adults to the cities in the hope of finding jobs.

7

"A virtuous wife is a man's best treasure. The most perfect Muslims are those whose disposition is best; and the best of you are those who behave best with their wives. Paradise lies at the feet of mothers."
–A saying attributed to Prophet Muhammad

A woman herds livestock in a rural village.

Egyptians living in the cities, especially those who are educated or wealthy, live a far more cosmopolitan life. Although urban entertainment, fashion, and food have been influenced by the West, religious (Islamic) beliefs and traditions remain the unifying factor that distinguishes the Egyptian lifestyle.

CHILDREN

Egyptians love children, and a big family is considered a blessing from God. In the past, there were very practical reasons for having a large number of children. As they grew older they could help with the family's work in the fields, and as adults they could look after their aged parents. Faced with a high infant mortality rate, people found it made sense to have as many children as possible in order to increase the probability of at least some surviving. Although these reasons are losing ground as more Egyptians adapt to urban environments and lifestyles, children continue to be a source of joy for families, even smaller urban families.

Two Nubian eight-year-olds sell souvenirs in Cairo.

Another perceived benefit of raising a big family is linked to a belief among the more traditional men that having many children, especially boys, makes them stronger.

Traditionally, it is the women in the family who take care of the children. The men do not spend as much time with the children as the women do, although the men do fuss over the children when they are together. A father may distance himself even more as the child grows older, sometimes thinking this necessary to maintain the child's respect.

Children in the countryside often have jobs at an early age. Before going to school they look after the family's animals. After school they do their homework, and then they help around the house or with the herd or crops. At harvest time, particularly in the cotton-growing areas of the Nile Delta, children work in the fields. Indeed, child labor is sometimes a problem in rural Egypt, and many children of poorer families work long hours to supplement the family income.

Attitudes toward children began to change in the 1960s, especially in urban society. Government action to improve the status of children in Egypt includes passing child labor laws that set the minimum age for agricultural employment at fourteen years. They also restrict the conditions in which children under age eighteen can be employed, provide compulsory education for children age twelve and younger, and implement programs with child welfare organizations. In addition, poor economic conditions have made people consider whether they have the financial means to support a large number of children.

EDUCATION

The Egyptian government provides free compulsory education for children until age fifteen. After six years of primary school, some children go on to three years of intermediate school and then another three years of secondary school. There are two kinds of secondary school: the general school teaches science, humanities, and mathematics, and awards the General Secondary Education Certificate, the equivalent of the U.S. high school diploma; the technical school trains students in specialized subjects such as agriculture and industry.

Egyptian students face fierce competition for places at institutions of higher learning. There are fourteen public universities, the largest being Cairo University in Giza. There are also four private universities, including the American University in Cairo. There are also several specialist institutes that offer courses in drama, ballet, film, and other subjects.

Egypt has greatly improved its education system in recent decades, raising the national literacy rate to about 82 percent for men and 66 percent for women. More than 90 percent of children enroll in school, but many drop out. To encourage attendance, the new school year does not start until after the cotton harvest. In primary school, which is compulsory and free,

children study mathematics, science, Islam, and Arabic. The government provides each child with a book for each subject. Students have to take regular exams, and the tests that determine whether they can climb to the next rung of the education ladder are particularly important.

However, despite all the effort the government has put into education, the system is struggling under the pressure of an increasing population.

Al-Azhar University, founded in 975 CE, is the center of Arabic literature and Islamic learning in Cairo.

Classes of forty-five children are not unusual in government-run schools; neither are dual sessions (morning and afternoon). Also, many teachers tutor privately after a full day at school to supplement their income, as public teaching does not pay well.

Many middle-class Egyptians send their children to private schools, with smaller classes of thirty. Before the 1952 revolution, there were more than 300 private schools in Egypt, many of which taught in French. Today, there are private schools in the country that teach in French, English, or Arabic.

EGYPTIAN NAMES

Many Egyptians give their children names from the Qur'an. Muhammad, being the name of the prophet who founded Islam, is by far the most popular boy's name, but other religious names such as Ahmad, Khalid, Mahmoud, Mostafa, Omar, and Osman are also very common among boys. Youssef is also popular. Fatimah, Eisha, and Shaimaa are examples of widely used religious names for girls.

There was a period after the 1952 revolution when the old Arabic names regained their former popularity. Egyptians born during the 1960s and 1970s are more likely to have names such as Wael, Walaa, or Waleed for boys, and Dalia, Liala, or Safa for girls. The trend now, however, is to go back to Qur'anic names.

MARRIAGE

Marriage is a very important part of Egyptian life and is encouraged by the Islamic faith. Marriage is not only the joining of two people but a union between two families that can support each other.

An Egyptian bride is surrounded by friends and family at her wedding celebration in Cairo.

In traditional Islamic society, there was little opportunity for young people to meet, so marriages were arranged by their families. This is still the case in the rural areas, where marriages are not only arranged within the village but are often made between cousins or other relations. Even in middle-class families, parents often make a lot of effort to introduce their teenage children to other teens who they feel will make good life partners.

There is little opportunity in the countryside for couples who are newly married to own their own home. Instead, the bride starts life with her husband in his family's home, where she is subordinate to both her husband and her mother-in-law until she has children and her status in the family rises.

In the cities, however, middle-class newlyweds in particular are no longer willing to live in their parents' home. A man may be expected to provide a furnished home that he can move into with his wife as soon as they marry. This means it could take him several years of earning and saving before he is sufficiently established to attract a bride.

The Egyptian wedding ceremony is very simple, a civil rather than a religious contract. All that is needed is the signing of a formal contract between the bridegroom and the bride's male guardian—usually her father, although it could be her brother or uncle. The contract must be signed in the presence of witnesses. In theory, any respectable Muslim man can act as witness. However, to make the marriage more official, the wedding party

visits a special office to acquire the service of a government witness called a *mazoun* (MAA-zoon). The contract usually refers to a sum of money called *mahr* (MAHR), which the groom gives the bride's family to buy furniture before the wedding.

After the service, it is important to announce the marriage, so there is a procession from the house of the bride's family to her new home. In the rural areas, a great feast follows the wedding. Virtually everyone in the village is invited to the feast; even the poorest family will give a big feast, even if it means going into debt to pay for it.

A Muslim bride and groom recite prayers at the mosque during a wedding ceremony.

Although Islamic law allows a man to have four wives, it is very unusual in Egypt, where monogamy is encouraged. Generally, a man will only take a second wife if his first wife cannot bear children or becomes ill. Egypt has a very low divorce rate, particularly in the rural areas where it brings shame to both families. When a married couple is facing problems, their relatives try to keep them together. The Qur'an discourages divorce. The Prophet Muhammad described it as "the most hateful of all permitted things." If a woman is widowed, she will often marry a second husband within the same family.

THE ROLE OF WOMEN IN SOCIETY

Women in Egypt enjoy greater legal equality with men than do women in many other Arab countries. Legally, they do not have to wear veils or traditional Islamic clothing. They vote, go to school, own property, and drive cars.

By Western standards, however, many Egyptian women lead restricted lives. Bearing the main responsibility of raising their children and looking after the home, women are less likely to have professional lives.

The government is trying to promote changes in the status and role of women in Egypt, and today many government organizations employ women as well as men in top management positions. For example, the state-run television and radio stations have both had women managing directors, and Egypt has sent several women ambassadors overseas.

The government can lead

Egyptian actress Elham Shahine sits in the office of her suburban Cairo apartment.

the way, but it is difficult to change the centuries-old attitudes of the people. In many households, the woman's place in the home is as restricted as it has always been. It is virtually unheard of for a woman to leave the protection of her family until she is married, and after marriage she is expected to submit to her husband. Single women do not go to the movies without a male family member. Women in the rural areas might never leave the village except to go to the market or a wedding.

Egyptian women have made great gains in education. The percentage of women with a secondary- or university-level education has more than doubled over the past two decades. However, the enrollment rate for girls remains lower than that for boys at all levels. Girls also have a higher dropout rate than boys. In many schools, boys are seated nearer the front of the classroom, where they receive more attention. Poorer families are certainly less likely to allow a daughter to go on to higher education.

Although traditional attitudes restrict women in many ways, they also give women certain rights and privileges. Even in the most traditional home, Egyptian women still exert great authority. It is the women who have control over money and legal papers, and who have a great say in the raising of the children.

THE URBAN MIDDLE CLASS

Today, more Egyptians than ever are living in cities. For the well-to-do, Cairo or Alexandria offers a high standard of living. The Egyptian middle class enjoys many amenities and comforts of modern living. For the not-so-well-to-do, city life offers better job opportunities than in rural areas and the hope of a better lifestyle.

However, city life comes with its own problems. Traffic congestion and pollution affect people's health. There are very few houses in Cairo, so even wealthy families live in apartments. There is no yard, but the apartment is large and comfortable and almost certainly has a balcony where the family can relax. The streets are busy, and children of middle-class families are not likely to be allowed to play outside, so they have to find ways to amuse themselves indoors.

Urban apartments in Egypt are likely to be filled with ornate furniture, and the television is the central feature of the living room. Few Egyptian wives work outside the home; most of them stay home to organize the house

Most city people live in apartment buildings like these in downtown Cairo.

and prepare the meals. However, this is changing, as younger women in middle-class families attend college or university.

Most middle-class families employ a maid who lives in the apartment. She looks after the children and does the chores. There may be another family living on the roof, in homemade accommodations. In that case, the family may be employed to keep the stairway tidy and do other small jobs for a small sum of money.

When urban families go out, it is usually to the shopping centers or to visit relatives. Those in Cairo who can afford the high entrance fee to the 614-foot (187-m) Cairo Tower might choose to enjoy a bird's-eye view of the city. After work and school, most families are often content to relax together over a meal and then watch television.

The Cairo Tower, also called Borj al-Qahira, is the tallest point in the city, with panoramic views out to the pyramids.

Egyptians can be very enterprising, and sometimes it seems that everybody in Cairo has two or three jobs. Even Egyptians in good occupations often need to have extra sources of income to cover their expenses. An army doctor, for example, may run a private practice in the evenings and may own an extra property in the city that is being rented out. An accountant may do private bookkeeping in the evening, own a share in a relative's shop, and occasionally drive a taxi.

FUNERALS

In Egyptian villages, when a member of the family dies, the women of the household start a ritual wailing. Their cries carry the news of the death to the rest of the village.

In all Islamic lands, the body is usually buried within twenty-four hours. (This is a sensible practice in countries that are generally very hot.) The corpse is washed, dressed in a shroud, and placed on a bier. The bier is then carried either to the mosque or directly to the cemetery. All the men of the family take turns carrying the bier, followed by a long procession. It is considered a good deed to join a funeral procession, even if the deceased was a stranger.

Superstition is deeply ingrained in Egyptian culture. The most common fear is of "the evil eye," which is a spell that brings bad luck. This belief may well relate to the pharaonic story of Horus, who had an eye pulled out in his fight with Seth. According to tradition, the evil eye can cause bad luck or sickness, but there are various ways to ward it off. God's name is often spoken out loud to give protection against bad luck; people may say "Bismillah" (BES-me-lah), which means "in the name of God," or "Ma Sha Allah" (MAH-shah-lah), which means "what God wills." People wear these expressions on charms and amulets. Other symbols worn to give protection against the evil eye include a blue bead, an open palm with the fingers spread out, or a representation of an eye.

In the past, infant mortality rates were high in Egypt, and the very young were considered particularly vulnerable to evil spells. Charms, or even a dirty face, were thought to give some protection, as did dressing the child as a sheik or monk, or in cloth begged from others. These practices continue even though infant mortality rates have improved.

The evil eye is usually associated with envy, and it is therefore impolite to openly admire someone else's possessions. In the more rural areas, this would be considered quite suspicious behavior. If people believe that they are the victim of a spell, there are several things they can do to break it. For example, they can smash an earthen jar behind the person they believe to be casting the spell. If a spell has caused illness, a paper doll is pricked with a needle and then burned, and the ashes are moved in circles over the sick person seven times before being thrown away.

Egyptians in the rural areas remain very superstitious, but even in the cities one still sees everyday examples of superstitions. For example, good luck charms dangle from the fenders of many motor vehicles. The charm often takes the form of an old shoe, and losing this talisman is believed to bring extremely bad luck. Many superstitious practices are now performed simply out of habit. Tradesmen or shopkeepers, for example, kiss and touch their forehead with the first piece of money that they receive each day as a sign of thanks and praise to God.

At the grave, an imam leads the mourning and recites prayers to God and to the Prophet Muhammad. This is followed by silent prayers and the burial. Muslims do not believe in cremation.

In the home of the deceased, the family will read the Qur'an for several nights and hand out food to the poor. Wealthier families may decide to hold a wake on the evening of the burial. Brightly lit tents are erected for this purpose and gilt chairs hired for the guests. A wake may block a major road, but nobody is likely to show disrespect by complaining. The mourners are likely to be entertained by a *maqri* (MAH-kri), a professional Qur'an reader. Some of the more famous readers enjoy a large popular following and have become rich from their performances. A wake can continue on successive Thursdays after the death, but an excessive show of grief may be frowned upon, as it is considered impious to protest the will of God.

INTERNET LINKS

egypttoday.com/

Egypt Today Magazine

This is an excellent, up-to-date English language site about modern Egyptian life.

www.cairotower.net/

Cairo Tower

This tourist information site offers panaramic views of Cairo.

www.egyptdailynews.com/

Egypt Daily News

This independent news site in English offers up-to-the-minute news about Egypt.

RELIGION

The beautiful and historic mosque of Abu Abbas al Mursi is the largest mosque in Alexandria.

8

I F THERE IS ONE COMMON THEME THAT has dominated Egyptian life from ancient to modern times, it is the vital role of religion. Egypt's religions have changed over the thousands of years of its history, but throughout, they have formed the very substance of Egyptian culture.

The ancient Egyptians worshiped many gods, such as Re, Hathor, and Anubis. One of the central themes of their religion was a belief in the afterlife, and people went to incredible expense to build tombs to house their bodies after death.

Visitors are dwarfed by the huge statues of the king Ramesses II at the Temple of Hathor and Nefertari at Abu Simbel.

• • • • • • • • • • •
"Provide dwellings for your people in Egypt, make your dwellings into places of worship, and establish regular prayers: and give glad tidings to those who believe!"
–from the Qur'an, (10:87), Jonah (Yunus)

The ancient Egyptian religion proved very resilient and survived well into the Roman period. The Roman emperor, Theodosius I, did not order the old temples closed until the end of the fourth century CE, and it is probable that the ancient gods continued to be worshiped in secret for some time after that. However, Christianity eventually swept away the Egyptians' ancient beliefs, and for three centuries Egypt was a Christian nation. The Coptic Christians still make up the largest religious minority in Egypt.

In 639 CE, Arabs, driven by their new religion Islam, conquered Egypt. There were considerable social and financial benefits for Muslim converts, and today Egypt is a predominantly Islamic nation. Most Egyptians are Sunni Muslims. Sunni Muslims constitute the majority (about 85 percent) of the world's Muslims.

Unlike some of its neighbors in the region, Egypt has never declared itself an Islamic state. For the past 150 years, Egypt has largely pursued a secular path, respecting Islam but generally separating religion as far as possible from the day-to-day workings of the state. Education is now run by the

While performing prayers, a man touches his forehead to the ground. Muslims pray five times a day.

state rather than the mosques. While Islamic law in principle is the sole source of legislation, Egypt's court system is chiefly secular and applies criminal and civil law based primarily on the French Napoleonic Code. In recent years, however, the influence of conservative Islamists has grown.

ISLAM

Islam is the second-most widely

A crescent moon, the symbol of Islam, adorns this small mosque in Hurghada.

practiced religion in the world today, after Christianity. Approximately 23 percent of the world's people are Muslims, or followers of Islam. They believe in one God, Allah, the creator of the universe and judge of humankind. Muslims believe that Muhammad is the final prophet, or messenger, "the last seal of the prophets," and that God's revelations to Muhammad complete the series of revelations to Jews and Christians.

The literal meaning of Islam is peace, submitting one's will for God's pleasure. The message of Islam was revealed to Prophet Muhammad 1,400 years ago through the angel Gabriel and was preserved in the *Qur'an* (sometimes spelled *Koran*), Islam's holy book. Muslims believe that the Qur'an carries a divine guarantee that safeguards it from being altered or corrupted, and that it combines the best features of the earlier scriptures.

The prime message of Islam is the unity of God, that the creator of the world is one and he alone is worthy of worship, and that Muhammad is God's messenger and servant. Muslims also believe in the angels, in God's previously revealed books, including the Bible, and in all the prophets from Adam to Jesus. (They believe Jesus to have been an important prophet, but not, as Christians believe, the son of God.) They also believe in the Judgment Day.

Muslims have five main duties: bearing witness to the unity of God and

ANCIENT GODS

The ancient Egyptians worshiped many gods who, they believed, influenced different aspects of everyday life. The gods were portrayed as human, animal, or a combination of both. Many of the gods were local to one town or district, but if the area prospered, the local god would gain wider popularity. For example, Amon progressed from being the sun god of Thebes to being the king of the gods to being associated with the sun god Re, from which time he became known as Amon-Re.

According to the beliefs of the ancient Egyptians, mummification was necessary to ensure a dead person's entrance to the afterlife. Once the person's soul had passed from the earthly realm it had to wait before the god Osiris and his forty-two judges as they weighed the person's heart against a feather. If the scales balanced, the deceased could enter the underworld and enjoy a peaceful afterlife; if the scales tilted, a monster would devour the heart, and the deceased would die a second, permanent death.

Spells, hymns, and prayers written by the ancient scribes were carved on the walls of pyramids from the fifth dynasty onward to help the kings in their journeys in the afterworld. The magical texts were eventually compiled into the Book of the Dead, a sacred funerary manuscript.

Everything a person needed in the afterlife was placed in the tomb. The pharaohs' tombs had thrones, war chariots, and chambers of gold items. To preserve the dead person for the afterlife, the body was mummified—its organs were removed and the body was dried out and then stuffed with resins and preserving oils, and then wrapped in strips of linen and placed in the tomb.

The ancient Egyptians regarded their kings as being partly human and partly divine. The pharaohs often associated themselves by name and symbolism with various gods. For example, the name of Seti I (father of Ramesses II) is connected to the name of the god Seth, and Amenhotep IV, whose name originally honored the god known as Amen or Amon, called himself Akhenaton in reference to the god Aton.

Priests had religious power second only to that of the pharaohs. The priests performed religious rituals, read the scrolls to the people, took care of the statues of the gods, and composed magical texts to help people in the afterlife.

 **ISIS** *Queen of the gods, sister and wife of Osiris. Portrayed as a woman with a throne on her head. She became popular in the New Kingdom.*

 **RE** *Sun god, king of the gods, father of humankind. He is shown as a man with a falcon's head and sun disk. He holds an ankh and scepter.*

 **ANUBIS** *The embalmer and god of the dead. He is shown as a black jackal or a man with a jackal's head.*

 **HATHOR** *Goddess of love, birth, and death. Portrayed as a woman with cow's horns and a sun disk. She holds an ankh and scepter.*

SETH *God of chaos, storms, and the desert. He is depicted as a man with an animal's head. He murdered his brother Osiris.*

 **THOTH** *Moon god, god of learning, inventor of writing. He is shown as a man with the head of an ibis wearing a crown.*

NEPHTHYS *Goddess of women, sister of Isis and Osiris, wife of Seth. She is depicted with a household object on her head.*

HORUS *Son of Isis and Osiris. God of the ruling pharaoh. He is portrayed as a man with the head of a falcon wearing a crown.*

OSIRIS *King of the dead. He was murdered by his brother Seth and resurrected by his wife Isis.*

PTAH *In Memphis, Ptah was believed to be the creator of the world. He was the patron of craftsmen.*

SOBEK *God of water, thought to have created the Nile from his sweat. He is portrayed with a crocodile's head.*

AMON *King of the gods, patron of the pharaohs. He is often identified with the sun god Re, as Amon-Re.*

Muhammad as His messenger; observing the prescribed prayers; giving to charity; fasting; and making a *hajj*, or pilgrimage, to Mecca. Mecca, in Saudi Arabia, is Islam's holiest city. Muslims pray five times a day, facing Mecca, at the mosque or wherever they are. Women usually pray at home; when they go to the mosque, they pray separately from men. Many Egyptians go to the mosque at least for the Friday noon prayer.

The Qur'an is the sacred scripture of Islam; Muslims believe that the book contains the words of Allah, as revealed to the Prophet Muhammad. Many Egyptians have a copy of the Qur'an at home, probably on a stand, never on the floor. The Qur'an has 114 chapters, known as *surah* (SOO-rah), each with its own name and varying in length from a few lines to several hundred verses. Adherents find the language of the Qur'an to be powerful and beautiful, especially when read out loud. The first surah, Al-Fatiha, is recited by devout Muslims every day as part of their prayers.

Muslims regard the Qur'an as the final and complete revelation of God; it cannot be altered. Translations of the Qur'an are widely available, but they are not used in official ceremonies or in prayers and rituals.

THE IMAM

Any Muslim man of good faith can lead the prayers at the mosque. A woman may lead the prayers only if there are no men in the congregation.

Besides leading the prayers, the imam might give lessons in the Qur'an and answer people's questions regarding the interpretation of Islamic laws. The imam is also expected to give a sermon on Friday after the prayers. This gives him considerable influence over his community, and most mosques appoint a trained imam. The Al Azhar Mosque, located in Cairo, has been a training center for teachers, missionaries, and religious judges for centuries and is today a university for religious studies.

The government approves major religious appointments and controls who is allowed to give sermons on television and radio. An imam who has a reputation as a dynamic or controversial speaker can draw thousands of people to the mosque. Popular sermons are recorded for sale.

It is the duty of every Muslim to visit the holy city of Mecca at least once in his or her life, unless prevented from doing so by poverty or illness. Every year, thousands of Egyptians make the pilgrimage, or hajj. *When they return to their villages, many pilgrims paint murals on the outside of their houses, showing scenes from their journeys. Apart from religious rituals, many of these murals include pictures of airplanes or passenger ferries. These paintings are a reminder that for many Egyptians the hajj may be the only chance they will ever get to see the outside world.*

The hajj is performed during the second week of the twelfth month of the Islamic calendar. At the start of the hajj, male pilgrims put on an ihram *(EE-rahm), which is made from two white sheets of seamless cloth. This symbolizes purity and makes all people equal, whatever their status or wealth. There is no prescribed dress for women, but they must go veiled.*

The pilgrims enter the haram *(HAH-rahm), the sacred area around Mecca that is forbidden to non-Muslims. At the Great Mosque, Muslims walk seven times around the Ka'bah, a 40-foot (12-m) long, 50-foot (15-m) high block of black granite that is the central shrine of Islam that all Muslims face when praying. Muslims believe that the Ka'bah marks the place where heavenly bliss and power directly touch the Earth.*

The pilgrims now perform the sa'y *(sah-EE), a ritual that involves running seven times between the hills of Safa and Marwah. Then the hajj moves to Mina, some five miles (8 km) east, for a time of prayer and meditation. Starting at midday, the pilgrims stand and pray on the plain of Arafat, where Muhammad preached his last sermon. The afternoon of prayer and meditation, which continues until just before sunset, is considered the supreme experience of the pilgrimage to Mecca.*

The pilgrims spend the night at Muzdalifah and then go back to Mina just before daybreak. They spend three days at Mina, throwing seven stones at each of three pillars each day. The throwing of the stones symbolizes the casting out of evil.

At the end of the hajj, the pilgrims sacrifice an animal as a gesture of renunciation and thanksgiving, and then distribute the meat to the poor.

COPTIC CHRISTIANITY

The Coptic Christians are the largest religious minority in Egypt. There is a particularly large concentration of Coptic Christians in central Egypt, around the city of Asyut. There are also large Coptic communities in Luxor, Cairo, and Alexandria. The number of Copts in Egypt is about seven or eight million.

Saint Mark the Evangelist is said to have brought Christianity to Egypt in the first century CE, several years after the death of Jesus Christ. There, he founded the Church of Alexandria. Persecuted by the Romans, many Christians sought refuge on the edge of the desert, where they lived as hermits. Later, they formed small religious communities. This monastic life is still an important part of Coptic Christianity today, and there are several large, active monasteries in Egypt, such as Saint Anthony's in the Arabian Desert near the Red Sea.

Christianity began to prosper in Egypt after it became the religion of the Roman Empire, and the Greek branch of the church was soon ruling over forty bishoprics in northern Egypt. A series of theological debates in 451 CE resulted in the Eastern Orthodox Church, of which the Egyptian Church is a part, breaking away from the Roman Catholic Church. The main issue was the

The interior of a Coptic church in Sharm el-Sheikh gleams with golden light .

essential nature of Jesus Christ: the Church of Egypt retained its belief in *monophysitism,* the belief that Jesus had a single, divine nature. The Church of Rome took the belief that Jesus was both divine and human. This difference still separates the Egyptian Coptic Church from the Roman Catholic Church.

Today Coptic Christianity has its own leader, or pope. The current Coptic pope, chosen in 2012, is Pope Tawadros II. Outnumbered by Muslims, Copts tend to maintain tight communities. In the past, they established their own schools, which today are open to anyone and may have many Muslim pupils. The Egyptian government has a policy of tolerance toward Christians, and there have been Christians in high office.

There are also a small number of Catholics and Protestants in Egypt, and they have their own churches. Sunday, the main religious day for Christians, is a work day in Egypt. So Christians are allowed time off from work on Sunday to go to church. Churches normally have two services, one in the morning and one in the evening.

Music forms an important part of church services, and there are hymns in Arabic (the official language of Egypt) as well as in Coptic (the traditional language of the Copts). Coptic church services are the only opportunity for the use of the Coptic language in Egypt today.

A Coptic cross, the Coptic Christian symbol, stands at the entrance to the Orthodox Church in Hurghada.

INTERNET LINKS

www.bbc.co.uk/religion/religions/islam

BBC Religions: Islam

This is an easy-to-understand introduction to the religion and culture.

www.coptic.net/CopticWeb

The Coptic Network

This site is an excellent portal to the history and creed of this religious community as well as Egyptian life in general.

LANGUAGE

Hieroglyphics, the written form of the Egyptian language, transmit information through a combination of pictures and sound symbols.

9

THE ANCIENT EGYPTIANS SPOKE A language that today is called Egyptian. It's the oldest known language in Egypt, and one of the oldest written languages in the world. The language gradually evolved into a form that is still used in the Coptic Christian Church. Today's Egyptians, however, do not speak Egyptian.

They speak Egyptian Arabic. Arabic spread in the Middle East as Arab armies swept through the region in the seventh and eighth centuries CE. Arabic has become one of the world's major languages; it is the official language of twenty-six countries and some form of Arabic is spoken by about 230 million people. It is one of the six official languages of the United Nations, along with Chinese, English, Russian, French, and Spanish. It is also the language of the Qur'an and therefore has religious significance to millions of non-native Arabic speakers.

Arabic writing uses twenty-eight symbols and is read from right to left and from top to bottom. Many of the letters are flowing and circular. There's a long tradition of competitions in which sections of the Qur'an are copied out, so handwriting has become a respected art form. Indeed, the word calligraphy comes from the ancient Greek and means "beautiful writing."

There are many different scripts. Originally, the Kufic script that developed in the Iraqi city of Kufah was the most widely used. However, a relatively plainer script called Naskhi gained popularity. Today Naskhi

"Classical Arabic, being the language of the Qur'an, has not changed at all in fourteen centuries, making the writings of the early Islamic scholars as accessible today as they were then."
—Jim Al-Khalili, contemporary Arab scientist and author

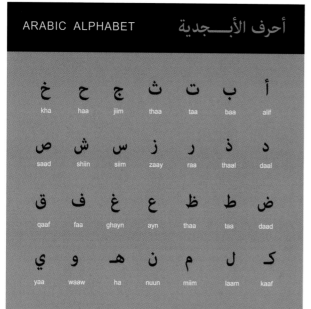

خ	ح	ج	ث	ت	ب	أ
kha	haa	jiim	thaa	taa	baa	alif
ص	ش	سا	ز	ر	ذ	د
saad	shiin	siim	zaay	raa	thaal	daal
ق	ف	غ	ع	ظ	ط	ض
qaaf	faa	ghayn	ayn	thaa	taa	daad
ي	و	هـ	ن	م	ل	ك
yaa	waaw	ha	nuun	miim	laam	kaaf

The names and shapes of the letters in the Arabic alphabet

is the main script used because it is very clear and ideal for modern printing. Other scripts are used for different purposes. Official documents may be printed in Diwani or Diwani Jali, both very ornate, formal scripts, which were brought to Egypt by the Ottoman Turks.

DIFFERENT FORMS OF ARABIC

There are many different written and spoken forms of Arabic. Classical Arabic, the language of the Qur'an, is described as a written language, although it may be used in speech, such as in sermons and plays. Novels written in a more modern form of Arabic may also use classical Arabic to record dialogue between characters.

Colloquial Arabic is significantly different from classical Arabic. There are nine major regional dialects, which differ in vocabulary, grammar, pronunciation, and syntax. Someone from Lebanon or Iraq may have difficulty understanding an Egyptian. Indeed, northern Egyptian and southern Egyptian are two separate and distinct dialects. Two Egyptians meeting for the first time can tell whether the other is from Cairo, in the north, or Upper (southern) Egypt by the way each of them speaks, although they would have no problem understanding each other.

Because of these regional differences, a third form of Arabic is developing in Egypt that is simpler than classical Arabic and that avoids the problems of colloquial Arabic. This third form, sometimes called Modern Standard Arabic, is understood throughout the Arab world and is used by the leaders of different Arab nations whenever they meet. Its written form appears in newspapers, formal documents, and works of nonfiction, while its spoken form is increasingly heard on radio and television and in formal speeches.

Modern literary Arabic has always used the Qur'an as a guide and has therefore stayed quite close to classical Arabic. Modern Arabic is more

> ## ARABIC WORDS IN ENGLISH
>
> *During the early spread of Islam, the Arab people were a dynamic force. Apart from being a great military power, they led the world in trade, science, and navigation. Just as today's English has given the whole world a computer vocabulary, so did Arabic lend many words to other languages some 800 years ago.*
>
> - *Arab astronomers named many stars, such as* Altair, Algol, *and* Aldebran.
> - *Arab traders brought the words* satin, cotton, sequin, tariff, saffron, *and* caraway.
> - *Arab mathematicians provided the words* algebra *and* average.
> - *Arab chemists gave the words* alcohol *and* alkali.

similar to classical Arabic than many other present-day languages are to their predecessors. So Arabs today would probably have less trouble reading an ancient classical manuscript than English-speakers might have understanding a text written in Middle English. (That is the form of English that was used from about 1150 CE to 1500 CE. It is significantly different from Modern English.)

COLORFUL EXPRESSIONS

Arabic is a colorful and expressive language. Daily conversations are filled with popular phrases, many with a religious meaning, that communicate a sense of gratitude and generosity. For example, *al Hamdulillah* (al HAHM-du-lee-lah) means "praise be to God," as in, "Our plane arrived safely in Cairo, al Hamdulillah." The phrase *insha Allah* (een-SHAH AWL-lah) means "if God wills it," as in "My car will be ready tomorrow, insha Allah." If a driver crashes into a wall and gets out safely, he or she might say, "*Maalehsh* (MAH-lesh)," which means "it doesn't matter," "too bad," or "don't take it seriously." This is partly to save face, but also acknowledges that things could have been worse.

Egyptians have other colorful expressions for greetings as well. For example, when someone wishes another person "Good morning," he or she may answer, "Morning of light." The first person may then reply, "Morning of jasmine." And this will probably be followed by a series of questions about

A street sign in Cairo uses Arabic and English.

each other's health and family. But no matter what the truth may be, it is customary to say that everything is wonderful—ending most statements with "al Hamdulillah."

THE PROBLEMS WITH TRANSLATION

Arabic does not translate particularly well into other languages. Since it uses a unique script and alphabet, there are often disagreements about how certain words should be spelled. So when naming Egyptian people and cities using the Roman alphabet, print media have to choose one of two or more possible spellings for the same Arabic name. For example, *Asyut* can also be spelled *Assiut*; *Fayyoum* and *Fayyum* are the same place; and the soccer player *El Khatib* may find his name spelled *Al Khatib*.

One source of confusion is the absence of many Arabic letter sounds in spoken English. For example, some Arabic letters indicate a strong guttural sound, a kind of gargling effect made deep in the throat. Different systems of translation use different letters, combinations of letters, and punctuation and accent marks to represent Arabic letter sounds in the Roman rendering.

Generally, provided the text you are referring to uses the accepted spelling for Arabic words, if you see the letter *k*, it probably sounds like "k" in English, while the letter *q* may sound either like "k" at the back of the throat or like "g," or it may be a silent letter. A combination of *g* and *h* (*gh*) may sound like the French rolled "r."

Translation becomes even trickier when considering regional dialects. Different regions may pronounce the same Arabic letter differently. Also, Arabic letters are mostly consonants; there are hardly any symbols to represent vowel sounds in written Arabic.

Learning a foreign language is becoming increasingly important for young Egyptians. Traditionally, wealthy Egyptians would learn French; but today English is considered the most important language to know. Recognizing the importance of foreign language skills in opening up career opportunities in other countries, university students might take some of their courses in English or French, rather than in Arabic.

Egypt's continuing efforts to speak with the rest of the world is vividly reflected in the new, state-of-the-art *Bibliotheca Alexandrina* (The Alexandria Library), which has a wall etched with alphabets from nations both ancient and modern.

HIEROGLYPHS: ANCIENT WRITTEN LANGUAGE

The Egyptian hieroglyphic writing system was first developed around 3000 BCE, with symbols to represent objects and actions. The word *hieroglyph* means "sacred carvings." The ancient Egyptians called the hieroglyphs "the words of the gods." Some hieroglyphs represent sounds; others represent concepts. Eventually more than 5,000 signs were created, although many were only occasionally used. The size of the hieroglyphic vocabulary made the language very difficult to master, and over time its use became limited to carvings on monumental tomb and temple walls.

A specially-trained scribe draws hieroglyphs in a museum.

Much of Ancient Egypt was still a mystery before the nineteenth century. There was a whole world of information carved on tomb walls or written on papyrus, but this was in a forgotten language that no living person understood. Most written information came from the early Greek travelers, whose notes and books people could still read and translate. However, there was only a tiny amount of such information, which had been written long after the ancient Egyptian civilization had gone into decline. The secrets of Ancient Egypt remained out of reach.

Then in 1799 an officer in Napoleon Bonaparte's army made a wonderful discovery outside the town of Rosetta. It was a slab of black stone that had three types of writing carved into it: the first two were the ancient Egyptian scripts, hieroglyphic and demotic; but the third was Greek, a language people still understood.

For the first time in history, scholars had a key to unlock the written treasures of ancient Egypt. However, the task was not easy. It was like having one page of a book in English and a copy of the same page in French, and having to learn the entire French language from that.

The man credited with breaking this ancient code is Jean-François Champollion, a French scholar born in 1790. By age eleven, he had taught himself most of the European languages. At eighteen he was a professor of history at Grenoble University in France. The Rosetta Stone became his great challenge.

By comparing the Greek with the Egyptian text, he worked out some of the meanings and sounds of the ancient language. He also understood Coptic, a language related to the earlier demotic and hieroglyphic languages, and this knowledge enabled him to decipher other words.

However, it was not until 1822 that Champollion managed to translate the complete text and publish his findings, which finally unlocked the lost world of Ancient Egypt for modern people to explore.

In addition to hieroglyphs, a cursive form of writing known as Hieratic was used by the ancient Egyptian scribes. Its signs are derived from hieroglyphic counterparts, but are more simplified and much quicker to write. Around the seventh century BCE, a new form of writing emerged. This script is known as demotic and was an even more cursive and abbreviated writing style. However, the Egyptians continued using hieroglyphs for important religious inscriptions until around 400 CE. The use of hieroglyphs died out during the later part of Roman rule.

The ancient scribes belonged to a highly honored profession, and wealthy people sent their sons to school to learn the written language. Students spent hours copying out hieroglyphs on papyrus, using pens made from reeds and ink made from a mixture of soot and water.

An oval with a horizontal line at the bottom, called a *cartouche*, indicates a royal name. This is the name of Pharaoh Thutmose III.

INTERNET LINKS

www.pbs.org/empires/egypt/special/hieroglyphs/introduction.html

PBS, Egypt's Golden Empire: Hieroglyphs

This section of the site, which is a companion to the video of the television series, is a fun, interactive introduction to hieroglypics.

www.arabic-language.org

This site features the Arabic alphabet, phrases, history, and more.

www.omniglot.com/writing/arabic.htm

Omniglot is an online encyclopedia of writing systems and languages.

www.al-bab.com

Select "Arabic Language" under Special Topics heading.

ARTS

Water pipes at a traditional market in Cairo display fine craftsmanship.

EGYPT'S ARTISTIC TRADITION DATES to the very beginnings of human culture. The paintings, sculptures, metalwork, and architecture of the ancient Egyptians are among the world's most magnificent treasures. The great museums of art, history, and culture—such as The Metropolitan Museum in New York, the British Museum in London, and the Louvre in Paris—all boast superb collections of ancient Egyptian arts and artifacts. Cairo's own Egyptian Museum contains the world's most extensive collection of pharaonic antiquities, including the treasures of King Tut's tomb.

The ancients transformed everyday items and translated figments of the imagination into works of beauty. With great vision and precision, they shaped and textured interesting yet practical pots and jars, sculpted grand images of the gods, decorated pyramids and coffins with meaningful symbols, and designed elaborate jewelry using precious stones and metals.

The arts remain an important part of Egyptian culture today. Over

10

Egyptian writer Taha Hussein supervised the translation of the complete works of Shakespeare into Arabic. In 1973 he was awarded the United Nations Human Rights Prize.

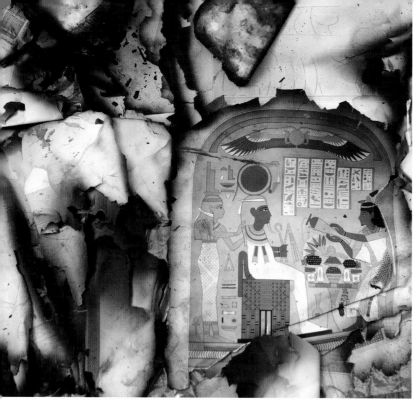

the last 150 years, however, Egyptian art has been greatly influenced by the Western world, as modern Egyptian painters, novelists, musicians, and filmmakers combine Western styles with ideas and emotions from their own experiences and culture.

ANCIENT LITERATURE

Probably only about 2 to 5 percent of Egyptians were literate during pharaonic times. Yet Egypt had a rich literary scene during the Middle Kingdom (1980—1630 BCE), considered the classical era of ancient Egyptian literature: poems, songs, stories, and instructional texts on a range of subjects, such as magic, mathematics, medicine, and astronomy.

Much of ancient Egypt's poetry is religious, some similar in style to the psalms in the Bible. There are complex stories with gods and goddesses, and various genres found in some texts. The ancient writers used puns, similes, and metaphors, and paid attention to presentation as well. Ancient Egyptian script was normally written from right to left, but for artistic purposes it could also be written from left to right or from top to bottom.

MODERN LITERARY FORMS

Under the influence of Arabic, folktales and narrative essays called *makama* (MEKH-ah-mah) became popular. However, poems retained their importance, as they were written for the common people. One of Egypt's best-known poets is Amal Dunqul (1940—1983), whose works focus on his country's political experience and connect with the sentiments of the nation, especially in the 1960s and 1970s.

Many writers have also turned their attention to novels, adapting this Western concept to develop their own story-writing style. Some of the earliest Egyptian novels looked at Western influences on Egypt. Tawfiq al-Hakim's *The Bird from the East* and Yahya Haqqi's *The Lamp of Umm Hashim* are good examples.

One of the earliest important books to look at life in the Egyptian countryside was Muhammad Husayan Haykal's *Zaynab,* published in 1913. Taha Hussein gained fame with his autobiographical novel, *An Egyptian Childhood*, in 1929. Born in a village and blind from age three, Hussein nonetheless made outstanding contributions to education and the arts in his country.

Some say Naguib Mahfouz is Egypt's greatest writer. He won the Nobel Prize for literature in 1988 for *The Cairo Trilogy*, the first Arab writer to receive that honor. Another internationally acclaimed author is Nawal El-Saadawi. Her works, including *The Fall of the Imam* (1987), provoked controversy in her home country and have been banned there.

Avid readers explore racks of books at the annual Cairo Book Fair.

MOVIES

Cairo is known as the Hollywood of Arabia, and Egypt produces a thousand or more movies a year for distribution throughout the Middle East.

The Cairo International Film Festival (CIFF) began in 1976, the first of its kind in the Middle East. Featuring acclaimed films from around the world, the event is the place to be for the Arab world's filmmakers. Celebrities from Hollywood have also made guest appearances at the Cairo festival. Alexandria hosts its own international film festival as well.

The political upheaval of 2013 and 2014 temporarily put the festival on hold, as well as the Egyptian movie industry in general.

THEATER

Egypt's only traditional theatrical art form is the puppet shadow play, called *khayal al-zill*, or "shadows of fancy." Performers use sticks or strings to move paper or leather puppets behind an illuminated white screen so that the audience sees only the moving shadows of the puppets on the screen.

Puppet shadow plays go back as far as 700 years ago and are still performed in Cairo. They normally consist of just one act, and the stories may be based on history or folklore—full of wit, humor, and plenty of action.

Egypt's simple folk plays originated in the villages, but modern drama is an import. Professional theater in the Middle East started in Syria during the nineteenth century. Political persecution by Turkish authorities forced many troupes to flee to the safety of Cairo. Salim Khalil al-Naqqash was one of those political refugees. In 1878 he wrote *The Tyrant*, the first play ever performed in Arabic. Around that time, Ya'qub ibn Sanu made a major contribution to Cairo theater with his comedies and operettas. He was the first of the early playwrights to use the colloquial dialect rather than classical Arabic.

The best known of all modern Egyptian playwrights was Tawfiq al-Hakim. As a young man he went to Paris to study law, but spent much of his time in theater and musical performances. When he returned to Egypt, he built a reputation as one of Egypt's most exciting and original writers. He wrote plays such as *The Bargain*, which paid tribute to the Egyptian fellahin. Although he usually wrote in classical Arabic, Hakim often used Egyptian folk dances and songs, which tended to be in colloquial Arabic, to make his work familiar to the common people.

Shadow puppetry is a very old art form; one that is found in many Asian cultures, as well as in Egypt.

BELLY DANCING

When Westerners think of belly dancing, they usually think of an exotic woman dancing alone before an audience. She wears a sheer, flowing costume that reveals her bare midriff, and she moves sensuously, rippling the muscles of her torso in time to the music. This style of dance, called raqs sharqi, *was introduced to Americans at the 1893 Chicago World's Fair, and came to be dubbed "belly dancing." At the time, many Americans considered the dance—and dancers—to be scandalous and improper, but it attracted enthusiastic audiences all the same. Today, many American women take belly dancing lessons for fun and exercise.*

The dance originated in the Middle East, possibly in Turkey. It has come to be most closely associated with Egypt—especially the Ghawazi people, a subset of the Dom, an Egyptian minority group sometimes called "gypsies." Many Egyptians hold the Ghawazi in low esteem, and particularly object to female performers showing their bodies. Indeed, it has been illegal in Egypt since the 1950s for belly dancers to perform publicly with their midriff exposed, and state-run television is forbidden to air the dance. In Cairo, belly dancers cater mainly to the tourist trade. Many Egyptians nevertheless enjoy the dance and will hire dancers for private parties and celebrations.

Another form of this dance style, raqs baladi, *is a more socially-acceptable folk dance. It is performed by both Egyptian men and women, in everyday clothing, at festive occasions such as weddings.*

MUSIC AND DANCE

Music and dance were important art forms in ancient Egypt. The early Greek travelers praised the beautiful songs and hymns of the Egyptians. Musical instruments were usually played to accompany the singer's voice and the dancer's movement. The most popular instruments at first were harps and flutes, but the New Kingdom Egyptians either invented or imported lutes and clappers.

The Arabs brought their own musical instruments, some of which the Egyptians already knew of. The lute became the most important instrument, although the viola, tambourine, and drum, and a fiddle called *rabab* (rahb-EUB) were also used. Sports and the fine arts received little attention from the Arabs, who developed music into the main art form.

The music of the Arab period can be divided into classical and folk. Classical music was used in the mosques for religious ceremonies and remained strict and formal; folk music was simpler and freer, making it easier to adapt.

Egyptian superstar Tamer Hosny performs at the site of the Giza pyramids.

Both have become familiar to the common Egyptian; a farmer in the fields might sing an age-old folk chant as well as a classical piece heard at the mosque.

Like many traditional art forms, both classical Arabic music and folk music in Egypt are being influenced by Western music. Even villagers have radios, and most Egyptians recognize the sounds of famous American or European musicians. In fact, the best of modern Egyptian music is often considered to be that which combines Western influences with traditional Egyptian sounds. Sayed Darwich, whose work blends classical Arabic music with European opera, is known as the father of modern Egyptian music. Mohammed Abd El Wahab has done a similar job of combining European pop with elements of Egyptian folk music. One of the biggest Egyptian pop stars today is Tamer Hosny, a Cairo-born singer, songwriter, producer, and director who blends Western and Arab instrumentation.

Perhaps the most famous Egyptian singer of all time was Umm Kulthum. More than a vocalist who sang to music played on traditional Egyptian instruments, she was an icon who spoke for Arabic music and musicians. When she died in 1975, millions of people joined her funeral procession through the streets of Cairo.

Egyptian folk dance is closely linked with traditional Egyptian music. Folk dances were originally developed to celebrate the stages of the agricultural cycle, and they were also performed at weddings or festivals. The dances vary from region to region, with the most distinctive ones coming from the far south and the oasis regions.

MODERN ART

Arabs have little tradition for the fine arts. However, there is an Egyptian School of Fine Arts, and the government encourages fine arts exhibitions and competitions.

Mahmoud Mokhtar (1891—1934) is the best-known modern Egyptian artist; many of his imaginative sculptures are displayed in his own museum in Cairo. One of the women pioneers of the modern art movement was Inji Aflatoun (1924—89). The Egyptian Museum of Modern Art in Cairo displays the works of Egyptian artists from the twentieth and twenty-first centuries.

A weaver creates one of the famous tapestries in the renowned school at Harrania.

FOLK ART

Egypt has a wealth of folk art, which, unlike the Western-style fine arts, is a natural outgrowth of its culture.

WEAVINGS The Wissa Wassef weaving school at Harrania, near Giza, produces extraordinary and exciting tapestries. The founder, Ramses Wissa Wassef, began with an isolated group of Harraniyyah villagers, who got their ideas and inspiration from their environment. Animals and landscapes feature in nearly all the Wissa Wassef tapestries. Each piece may take months to complete, and the colors and style often reflect the mood of the artist.

The Wissa Wassef weavers produce highly prized works. Wissa Wassef tapestries hang in some of the greatest museums in the world.

For centuries, Egyptian artists have made everyday objects decorative, partly to make them pleasing to the eye, but also to turn them into investments. The traditional materials used by these folk artists are brass, copper, ivory, silver, and gold. Wood is seldom used, simply because Egypt does not have any forests. Cottage industries flourish, and artisans use traditional skills passed down through generations to transform raw materials into works of art.

COPPER AND BRASS Although the sheets of metal are now produced in factories, copper and brass objects are still hammered out by hand in small family workshops. Mirror frames, trays, plates, vases, coffee pots, and smoking pipes are the most common objects manufactured. Tourist souvenirs such as name plates and Christmas tree ornaments are also being produced.

When damp, copper becomes toxic, so an item intended to be used in cooking should be lined with tin or silver. To make the metal more durable and easy to work with, it is often mixed with other metals. Brass, a common working metal, is a combination of copper and zinc. It has a golden color that makes it popular for decorative pieces. To make the items more attractive, they might be embossed, chased, or inlaid.

INLAID WORK Wooden chessboards, boxes, and chests are decorated with tiny pieces of mother-of-pearl laid into the wood to form mosaic patterns. Ivory was also once used for such work, but is now considered too controversial as well as expensive. Many nations ban the sale of ivory because of the great danger the ivory trade poses to elephants.

JEWELRY Many rural Egyptians have little knowledge of or faith in banking and prefer to invest in gold or silver. This is kept in the form of jewelry, and has created a whole industry to design and manufacture decorative items. The villagers favor large and bulky items, and this style influences even modern designs. Earrings, necklaces, and bracelets are the most common pieces. Other influences have come from Arabic calligraphy and tourist demand for pharaonic reproductions.

In some Egyptian cultures, women wear their wealth on their bodies in the form of gold jewelry.

INTERNET LINKS

www.saudiaramcoworld.com/issue/199902/shadows.of.fancy.htm

Saudiaramco World magazine online

This features a nice article about shadow puppets in Egypt.

www.sis.gov.eg/En/

State Information Service "Your Gateway to Egypt" (click on "Culture & Arts")

This government site features a wide range of topics about Egyptian music, art, theater, literature, movies, and more.

www.wissa-wassef-arts.com

The Ramses Wissa Wassef Arts Centre

The site has images of many weavings, as well as information about the artists and the history of the school.

www.puppet.org/museum/passports_elrekhim.shtml

The Center for Puppetry Arts

This site has information about many kinds of puppetry. This page focuses on Egyptian shadow puppets, including a video.

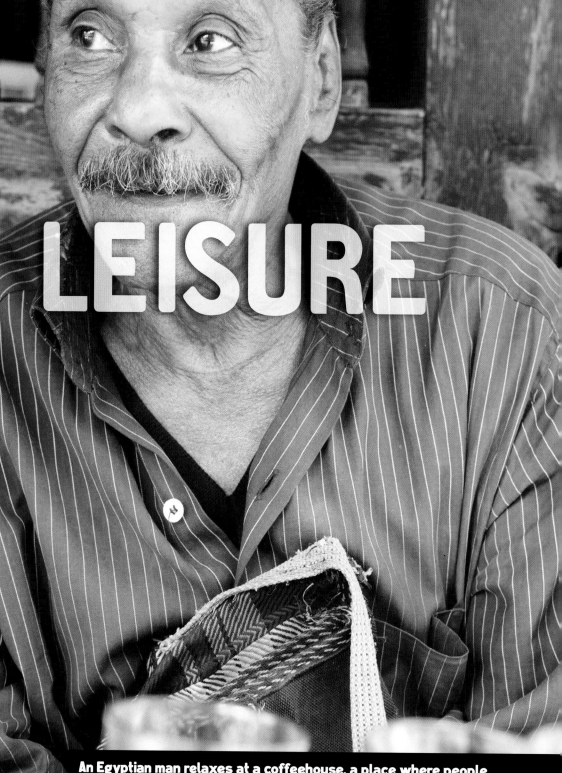

LEISURE

An Egyptian man relaxes at a coffeehouse, a place where people gather to meet friends and unwind.

11

RELAXING IS ONE OF THE MOST popular pastimes in Egypt. The hot desert climate—and manual labor in rural areas—have made people value any free time they can get just to sit somewhere and talk with friends. In the villages, a group of women may gather in the courtyard of one of their homes to chat; most men are likely to spend at least a few evenings in a coffeehouse.

THE COFFEEHOUSE

A typical Egyptian coffeehouse is a large, tiled saloon that is often crowded and alive with activity—coffee bubbling and glasses clinking, waiters squeezing between tables, shoeshine boys hovering, people laughing, dominoes clacking, dice rolling, and cards slapping. In most coffeehouses, the patrons are only men—although in some areas of Cairo and other modern cities, women may be present as well.

Going to a coffeehouse is a social activity, and people usually go with friends. There is a cheerful exchange of news and views among patrons at a coffeehouse, where the country's well-developed art of conversation is put to practice. People are admired for their wit and humor, as they weave proverbs and religious quotations into a discussion of local, national, and international events. In coffeehouses in rural areas, one

Just like American teens, Egyptians teens love to hang out at fast-food restaurants. Cairo has many American fast-food chains, such as McDonald's, Pizza Hut, Subway, and Chili's, as well as pizza places, Chinese take-out, and many Egyptian-style fast-food places.

Amina El Sergany referees a beach volleyball match at the 2012 Summer Olympic Games in London.

patron may read aloud from the newspaper to interested listeners.

Many coffeehouses, called *ahwas*, cater to a particular group of people, depending on their location, environment, and service. Some may attract fellahin, others intellectuals; some may be a favorite hangout for young people, others the preferred haunt of retired army officers.

A NATION OF SPORTS LOVERS

Egypt has a long history as a nation of sports lovers. Ancient Egyptian art shows sports such as wrestling, marathon running, and swimming. Except for the ice and snow sports, Egyptians play all the popular games from around the world. Most schools in Egypt have at least a small courtyard, where students play friendly basketball and volleyball matches or train for inter-school games. Working adults may engage in sports with friends in their leisure time. Watching competitive games is, of course, a popular alternative to actually playing them.

Egypt's first professional sports were wrestling and weightlifting. At the 1928 Olympics in Amsterdam, weightlifter Nasser El Sayed broke the world record and won Egypt's first-ever Olympic title. Egypt continued to bring home Olympic weightlifting medals from Berlin in 1936 and London in 1948, but lost out to other countries in subsequent meets.

At the 2012 summer Olympics in London, Egypt sent one of its largest delegations ever—109 athletes, seventy-five men and thirty-four women. They participated in eighty-three events across twenty sports and took home two medals.

Other popular water sports are rowing and sailing. Egyptians sail yachts at Al-Maadi, just a few miles south of Cairo, or in the open sea at Alexandria.

WOMEN AND SPORTS

For the 2012 summer Olympic Games in London, Egypt sent thirty-four female athletes, its largest delegation of women in the country's Olympic history. This is a sign of shifting attitudes and changing times.

Only recently has it become socially acceptable for young women in middle-class families to play sports such as tennis and squash. Girls may enthusiastically practice gymnastics and swimming, and some of the big sports clubs stage "women's only" afternoons in the gymnasium or pool, where women's sportswear can be worn without conflicting with local dress codes.

While women in Egypt are slowly being encouraged to take part in recreational sports, in many parts of the country it is still not considered normal for women to take sports seriously. Egyptian women who train as professional athletes face serious social pressures, such as chauvinistic attitudes, conservative dress codes, and traditional perceptions of gender roles (that women should marry young and start a family). Training for a career in sports may be viewed by society as conflicting with these expected duties and behaviors.

Those ideas are being challenged by female sports activists such as Sahar El-Hawary. She was the first female member of the Egyptian Football Federation, president of the first Arab league for women's soccer, or football as it is called internationally, and the first women's referee in North Africa. In 2003, she was the first Arab woman to be named the International Olympic Committee's Woman of the Year in Sports. In the 1990s, she formed a women's football team and built it into a league. El-Hawary considers her work nothing short of a revolution. Egypt is a country where most people think playing soccer is a game for men only. For women, traditionalists insist, playing the game is strictly haram, *or "forbidden."*

Egypt also has very good javelin throwers. However, Egyptian track athletes have yet to match the speed and stamina of North African runners, who are ranked among the best in the world.

By African and Middle Eastern standards, Egypt can produce strong teams in hockey, tennis, volleyball, handball, water polo, and basketball, and Egyptian squash players have won world tournaments.

Apart from winning regional events, Egypt has played a leading role in developing sports in Africa and the Middle East. For example, Egypt regularly hosts regional championships. The biggest event in Egypt so far was the 1991 African Games, an Olympic-like meet for teams from all over Africa.

FOOTBALL (SOCCER): A NATIONAL PASSION

Football is the undisputed king of Egyptian sports. (It is not the American game of football, but rather the sport Americans call soccer.) When a big match is played at the national stadium, the streets of Cairo are deserted, and everyone who is not at the stadium is probably at home, watching the game on television. Fans may react wildly to their favorite team's loss, damaging buildings close to the stadium, and tempers often flare up among the players themselves. However, when the Egyptian national team scores an important victory in an international game, the whole country celebrates, and cars drive around the streets with flag-waving supporters sitting on the roofs.

Though Ancient Egyptian art shows athletes playing a game resembling football, it was actually introduced to Egypt by the British in the nineteenth century. The Egyptians soon learned the game, and by 1907 they had their own club, Al Ahly. The Egyptian Football Association was founded in 1921 to develop the sport in Egypt. In the Olympic tournament in Amsterdam in 1928, Egypt beat Turkey, Portugal, and Argentina to get through the semifinals. The only other time Egypt made it to the semifinals was in 1964 in Tokyo.

Egypt helped to establish a regular football meet for African nations during the 1950s, and the African Football Confederation is still based in Cairo. The trophy of the African Nations Cup was donated by an Egyptian army officer, General Abdelaziz Mustapha, and the Egyptian team has won

the trophy four times since 1957. Since then, Egypt has participated in several African, Arab, Asian, and international championships. So far, its team has made it to the World Cup only twice, in 1934 and 1990, but did not win at either one.

At home, the favorite club is Al Ahly, which nearly always wins the Egyptian League. Zamalek, another Egyptian team (and Al Ahly's great rival), usually puts up a tough fight. Club colors are very important to soccer fans, who often go to matches wearing the same jerseys as the players on their favorite teams. Many Egyptian teams are owned or sponsored by large companies.

Egyptian fans cheer at an opening match of the FIFA World Cup tournament.

INTERNET LINKS

www.sis.gov.eg/En/

State Information Service of Egypt

Choose "society" and then "Egyptian sports."

www.aquila-style.com/focus-points/muslimah-turns-heads-in-olympic-beach-volleyball

This is a fun pop culture site for Muslims.

www.npr.org/2012/05/23/153512361/soccer-pioneer-builds-her-own-revolution-in-egypt

National Public Radio

This page features a story about Sahar El-Hawary.

FESTIVALS

A Sufi man performs the "whirling dance," a religious ritual of ecstatic devotion.

WHAT WOULD LIFE BE WITHOUT holidays? Most cultures observe special days for reasons of religion, state, cultural heritage—or just plain fun. Egyptians are no different. However, Muslim holidays are mostly quiet, prayerful occasions without colorful decorations and merriment.

A Sufi musician plays a traditional instrument. Sufis belong to a branch of Islam focused on mystical experience.

The Cairo International Book Fair, which takes place every January, is the largest annual cultural event in the Middle East. The fair attracts publishers, authors, book retailers, and avid readers from across the Arab world.

However, since Egyptians love festivals as much as people in any country do, other holidays have been added to the national calendar over the years. The best example is the Prophet Muhammad's birthday. Now an important holiday in Egypt, it was not celebrated until at least 400 years after Muhammad's death.

Most Islamic holidays are based on the Islamic, or *Hijra* (HEZH-rah) calendar. It is a lunar calendar consisting of twelve months in a year of 354 or 355 days. As a result, the holidays are celebrated at different times of the year on the modern Gregorian calendar. Four of the twelve months are considered sacred, with Ramadan being the holiest. Islamic holidays are usually celebrated with extra prayers, sermons, lavish meals, and visits among relatives.

NATIONAL HOLIDAYS

The anniversaries of major events give Egyptians more opportunities to get together with their family and friends for a meal. National holidays are marked with special reports and features in the newspapers and on television, and schools and factories may organize formal or social events. Armed Forces Day used to be celebrated with a grand military parade, until President Sadat was assassinated at one. No national parade has been held since, although individual governorates may stage military shows. National Day, on July 23, celebrates the 1952 Revolution and is the most important of the secular holidays.

RELIGIOUS HOLIDAYS

RAMADAN Observance of the holy month of Ramadan is one of the five pillars of Islam. When Muslims fast, they do not eat or drink while the sun is up. Every day during Ramadan, they fast from sunrise to sunset. At the end of the day, they listen for the prayer call on the radio or television, or from the mosque, which announces the end of the day's fast.

To decide when the day's fast is over, the imam at the mosque holds up two pieces of thread, one white and one black. It is considered night and time to end the fast when he can no longer distinguish between the two colors. The muezzin then announces the end of the fast with a call to prayer. The streets become empty, as people go home to break the fast with their families. They have supper before going to bed, and just before daybreak they wake up for another meal before starting the new day's fast.

Egypt's hot climate makes it particularly difficult to get through the day without refreshment. People often feel very tired during the Ramadan month, and the whole pattern of life changes. Government offices slow down or even stop work altogether, and it is not unusual for office workers to take short naps right at their desks during lunchtime. Schools often close early so that the students can go home for an afternoon nap.

Not everyone has to fast. Young children, the sick, and the aged are excused. Travelers, soldiers on duty, and women who are pregnant or nursing need not fast during Ramadan, but they should try to make up for "lost" fasting days at a later time.

People are more diligent about saying prayers and reading scripture

The month of Ramadan ends with the sighting of the new moon. After the end of the fast is announced, the gaiety of Eid al-Fitr begins.

Members of a Bedouin tribe prepare for their *iftar*, or breaking of the fast, during the Muslim holy month of Ramadan.

during Ramadan. Indeed, most families try to read the entire Qur'an by the end of the month. There is usually a large gathering outside the mosques each evening during Ramadan, as people celebrate the end of another day of fasting. These crowds build up in numbers and excitement as the end of Ramadan approaches.

EID AL-FITR Eid al-Fitr is the most important holiday in Egypt. It celebrates the end of Ramadan, and in the days leading up to Eid al-Fitr, the airports and harbors are crowded with Egyptians returning from their work abroad to spend the holiday with their families in Egypt.

The end of Ramadan is also the time when Muslims give to the poor a percentage, usually 2.5 percent, of their wealth. This offering is called *zakat* (ZAH-khat), another pillar of Islam. It is not considered charity, but is an act of worship. Indeed, the name *zakat* means "purify," and it is meant to remind everyone that all wealth really belongs to God.

EID AL-ADHA This religious holiday, also known by its Turkish name of *Qurban Bairam*, marks the end of the holy pilgrimage to Mecca, yet another pillar of Islam.

The main feature of the celebration is the lavish feast. In the days leading up to the festival of Eid al-Adha, everyone who can afford to do so buys a sheep or goat and leaves the animal in the street outside the house to demonstrate the family's wealth and impress the neighbors. The animals are slaughtered on the seventieth day after Eid al-Fitr, and big feasts are held at the mosques. A third of the sacrificed animal's meat is given to the poor.

MUHARRAM Muharram, the Islamic New Year, marks the day Muhammad and his followers set out for Mecca from Medina. Muharram is New Year's Day for Muslims, but it is not celebrated with big parties the way January 1 is celebrated in the Western world. (However, Egypt does also seem to come to a standstill on the Western New Year's Day, with many people missing work to go out.) Muharram is a festival for the family, as Muslims get together with their families to share a meal and exchange gifts.

The legacy of ancient Egypt includes more than art. Modern Egyptians continue to celebrate a festival that has evolved from the Spring Festival of ancient times. The Spring Festival was the most important festival in ancient Egypt. It celebrated the rebirth of the earth after winter. The day also marked the start of the year, which would run through the agricultural cycle.

During the Spring Festival, people ate eggs, which were seen as a symbol of renewal after death. The practice of eating eggs as a special celebration was adopted by the Jews and Christians. It continues in the Christian world today with the making of Easter eggs.

The ancient Spring Festival is today known as Sham el-Nessim. This translates from the Arabic as "breathing of the spring air." Sham el-Nessim is a national holiday and is celebrated at the time of the Coptic Easter. Both Copts and Muslims celebrate the holiday, although it is particularly important to Copts. Sham el-Nessim probably bears little resemblance to celebrations that took place in ancient Egypt, but the eating of eggs has remained a tradition. Ordinary hens' eggs are used, but they are boiled in a coloring to dye them brown. Salted fish and onions are also traditionally eaten on this day and are thought to prevent disease. Many families rise very early to picnic by the Nile or in the countryside.

The ancient Egyptians had numerous other local festivals, such as the Festival of the Living Falcon and the Festival of the Victory of Horus. One of the most important events was the Festival of the Sacred Wedding, when the statue of Hathor was taken from the temple of Dendera and rowed 100 miles (160 km) south to Idfu to meet the statue of Horus. The festival reenacted the union of Hathor and Horus on the night of the rising of the new moon.

Egyptian Coptic Christians attend a midnight mass on Coptic Christmas Day, January 7.

The Islamic year has 354 days, following the lunar calendar. This means that the major festivals occur twelve days earlier each year when compared with the calendar used in the West.

COPTIC HOLIDAYS Coptic celebrations usually take place later in Egypt than corresponding Christian holidays in Europe. For example, Christmas is celebrated on January 7. Copts celebrate their religious holidays with church services and family gatherings. They pay particular attention to the saints, and large numbers of people visit once-remote monasteries on special saints' days.

SAINTS' DAYS In the past, saints' days were occasions for villages to stage elaborate celebrations. Events took place at fairgrounds with bright lights and blaring music, acrobatics, belly dancing, and camel racing. There was also a religious feast at the local mosque.

Saints' days celebrations are now more subdued, and many have died out altogether. The celebrations often led to riots and crime, so the police objected to them. The Islamic authorities supported the suppression of saints' days as such events were considered unorthodox and thought to have pagan links. The only saint's day that is widely celebrated is *Mawlid al-Nabi* (MOO-led ahl-NAH-bee), the birthday of the Prophet Muhammad himself. This is an important national holiday, when it is traditional to give children sugar dolls and sweet pastries.

MAIN HOLIDAYS IN EGYPT

NATIONAL HOLIDAYS
New Year's Day—January 1
Sinai Liberation Day—April 25
Evacuation Day—June 18
National Day—July 23
Armed Forces Day—October 6

ISLAMIC HOLIDAYS
Muharram—New Year's Day
Mawlid al-Nabi—Birthday of the Prophet Muhammad
Eid al-Fitr—The end of Ramadan
Eid al-Adha—The end of the pilgrimage

OTHER HOLIDAYS
Sham el-Nessim—varies

COPTIC HOLIDAYS
Christmas—January 7
Epiphany—January 19
Easter—varies
Annunciation—March 21
Feast of Virgin Mary—August 15

INTERNET LINKS

www.sis.gov.eg/En/
State Information Service of Egypt, Your Gateway to Egypt
Choose "Society" and then "Egyptian festivals."

www.timeanddate.com/holidays/egypt/
This is a listing of the dates of holidays in Egypt.

www.touregypt.net
Top Ten Festivals in Egypt (Home page)
This site features articles about the Spring Festival, Ancient Egyptian festivals, Ramadan, and more.

FOOD

Egyptians particularly love stuffed vegetables, such as peppers, tomatoes, grape leaves, zucchini, and eggplant.

EVERYONE LOVES TO EAT, ESPECIALLY when the food is delicious and family and good friends are together. In Egypt, mealtime is a social occasion. At a family gathering or a business meeting, a meal may consist of several courses and cups of coffee. Often the food takes second place to the conversation.

The fava bean is a staple ingredient in Egyptian cooking, and people sometimes call it "the poor man's meat." It's used in soups, mashed for a dish called *foul*-for which every cook has his or her own recipe-and *falafel*, a fast-food dish of spicy fried patties served in pita bread.

One of Egypt's most popular meals is *foul medames*, a dish of mashed fava beans with cumin, parsley, onion, garlic, and lemon juice.

DAILY MEALS

Egyptians may have as many as five meals a day. Breakfast, at least in the city, is usually a drink at home and some *foul* (fool)—a bean dish—and bread bought from a stall on the way to work. By mid-morning, most Egyptians will have had a light meal of bread with cold meats, pickles, or eggs, and coffee or tea.

For lunch, people in the rural areas might have bread, cheese, dates, and vegetables; meat and fish, which are more expensive than vegetables, are reserved for special occasions. There are several kinds of Egyptian cheese: soft, hard, pickled, and spicy. People in the cities can also choose from a variety of Western cheeses.

For people in the cities, lunch may consist of rice, a meat dish, and a salad. Bread and rice are the main staples in Egypt. Yellow saffron rice with boiled lamb is a typical main course, while rice boiled with milk and sugar makes a popular pudding for dessert.

The evening meal, usually eaten at home, may be rice with cooked meats and vegetables. There will also be bread and perhaps olives and salads. Poorer families may simply have bread and stew. Fresh fruit, especially red watermelon, is a popular way to close any meal.

A typical supper, eaten at around 10 p.m., consists of foul with perhaps fried vegetable balls or grape leaves stuffed with rice.

COMMON INGREDIENTS

Even the wealthiest people in Cairo use the same ingredients in many of their meals as do people in the poorer areas. Generally, Egyptians use fresh ingredients when cooking. Olive oil is used mainly for cooking, but it may also be mixed with spices and nuts to make a spread. Olives are a favorite, seldom used as a cooking ingredient but often served as a snack with bread and cheese. The most common Egyptian cheese, a soft white cheese similar to feta, is made from sheep's or goat's milk.

A good Egyptian cook uses a variety of spices, such as caraway seeds,

Thanks to the fertile waters of the Nile, the ancient Egyptians enjoyed a variety and abundance of food that would have been the envy of other early civilizations. Although there was always the danger of floods and famine, in good years Egypt was a land of plenty.

Many of the foods that the ancient Egyptians ate were the predecessors of foods that people living along the Nile today still enjoy. Then, as now, bread was probably the staple food; indeed, the ancient Egyptians were among the first people to learn how to make leavened bread. They had many different bread recipes, some flavored with spices or with fruit such as dates. The ancient Egyptians also discovered the art of brewing; they made beer from barley, wheat, or dates. Beer was consumed with most meals, perhaps because ordinary water was considered unsafe.

The ancient Egyptian gardens grew a wide variety of produce, including cabbages, celery, grapes, and onions. People cooked lentils in soups and stews, while poultry and fish were important parts of the diet. Cattle, oxen, and sheep were kept for meat and milk.

Cooking was done in mud ovens and roast pits, or over open fires. Tableware was made from clay, and the wealthier people had drinking cups made from metal. There were spoons and knives, but much of the food would have been eaten with the fingers.

Selection and preparation were very important processes in dealing with food. Food had more than dietary uses; it was also offered for the dead. Indeed, much of our information about diet in ancient Egypt comes from drawings in tombs. For example, there are images of great feasts where a whole ox was roasted. Since the royal tombs were given far more attention, today we have very little information about the food that the poor of ancient Egypt ate.

cumin, marjoram, saffron, and thyme, to season anything from vegetable soups to meat kebabs. Egypt is located on the ancient spice route between Asia and Europe, and today many towns in Egypt have entire markets that sell nothing but spices.

Certain vegetables feature prominently in Egyptian cuisine. Eggplant is a favorite. This dark purple vegetable, also known as aubergine, was introduced from India more than 1,500 years ago and has found its way into many Egyptian recipes. Eggplant is used

Cinnamon, in the foreground, and a wealth of other spices are offered in bulk at a market in Egypt.

to make a dip such as *baba ghannooj* (bah-bah GAH-nooj), or baked with grilled lamb or mutton to make *moussaka* (MOO-sah-kah).

Other popular vegetables in Egypt include cauliflower, cucumber, onion, spinach, and tomato. The green pods of the okra plant often form the base of stews and soups. Fava beans are used to make foul. They may be boiled, then pureed with onions and spices; or mashed with different spices and shaped into patties and deep fried. Chickpeas are mixed with lemon juice, olive oil, and various spices to make hummus, and eaten with pita bread. Wheat, widely grown in Egypt, is used in baking bread. Corn is a popular staple for the peasants.

Lentils play an important role in the Egyptian diet as well. They are among the oldest domesticated crops in human history and were eaten in the Middle East some 9,500 to 13,000 years ago. In Egypt, *kushari* is a very popular dish, made of lentils, rice, pasta, and tomato sauce. Egyptians also like lentil soups.

INFLUENCES OF OTHER CUISINES

Egyptian cuisine reflects a Turkish influence, part of the legacy of the Ottoman Empire, of which Egypt was a part for several hundred years. *Kebab* (KAY-bahb) and moussaka, for example, are basically the same in Egypt as in other countries around the eastern Mediterranean.

Egypt has inherited culinary influences from its other foreign rulers as well, and many Egyptian dishes have Greek or Syrian roots. In recent times, Egyptian food, especially in the cities, has also come under international influence. In Cairo today there are foreign-cuisine restaurants and American fast-food branches. On special occasions, middle-class Egyptians might dine in a restaurant that serves a foreign cuisine, but most Egyptians generally prefer their own food.

RELIGIOUS RULES AND ALCOHOL

Religion has had a big influence on Egyptian eating habits. Most Egyptians, being Muslim, do not eat pork, and meat has to be slaughtered in a special ritual. A Muslim who knows how to kill the animal according to Islamic law cuts the windpipe of the animal while invoking the name of God, acknowledging Him as the creator of all things. The meat is then considered *halal,* or "fit to eat."

Alcohol is forbidden under Islamic law; no Muslim should drink alcohol or sell it even to a non-Muslim. However, Egypt has a long history of beer-making. Beer was a popular drink in Ancient Egypt, as can be seen in writings dating back 5,000 years. The pharaohs and common people alike drank beer daily, and the brew, made from baked barley bread, was also used in religious ceremonies. Surprisingly, perhaps, Egypt still has a large brewing industry, and most restaurants list beer on their drink menu. Beer is also offered to guests at weddings and other family feasts. People are far stricter about the no-alcohol rule during Ramadan, when restaurants and hotels usually sell alcoholic beverages only to tourists.

MEAT

Egyptians eat mostly lamb and mutton. Beef is not as common, as the land is not suitable for raising cattle. Roasted pigeon is a delicacy in the Egyptian countryside; many rural households keep an elaborate dovecote, and when there is a feast a pigeon is roasted and served as the main course. Camel and water buffalo meat is popular in poorer homes.

Halvah is a popular sweet often made with sesame paste (tahini) and pistachios or other nuts.

Egypt's traditional source of seafood is the Mediterranean coast, but today the Red Sea has become another important source.

SWEETS

Egyptians like sweet foods. They may have their pastries and cakes after meals or with tea or coffee between mealtimes.

Halvah and baklava are popular in Egypt and in many other Middle Eastern and Mediterranean countries as well. *Baklava* is a pastry made from paper-thin sheets of dough, filled with nuts, and sweetened with honey. There are many variations of halvah and baklava; the differences lie mostly in the filling. Some of the pastries may be filled with dried fruit, such as dates, figs, or apricots, while others are filled or decorated with ground nuts, such as pistachios or walnuts. Baklava may be dipped in syrup or honey. The flavor of each sweet is identified by its shape. Halvah and baklava are sold in cake shops in most towns in Egypt. Large bakeries display twenty or more kinds of halvah and baklava that go by delightful names such as "lady's wrist" and "eat and promise." Bakers work nonstop to refill the trays as orders roll in.

Another popular Egyptian dessert is *basbousa* (bas-BOO-sah), a cake made from semolina flour, yogurt or milk, and butter or oil, baked until golden brown, and then covered with syrup.

DRINKS

Egyptians drink a lot of tea and coffee. They like strong tea, and drink it with milk in the morning and plain the rest of the day. Teas spiced with jasmine, rose, mint, or saffron are popular. Fresh sugarcane juice is a refreshing thirst quencher, and hibiscus leaves are used to make a drink called *karkadeh* (kahr-KAH-deh).

Coffee is the national drink. Egyptians drink coffee after meals, when they visit people's homes during the day, and at cafés after work. There are two ways of serving coffee in Egypt: the Arab way and the Turkish way. Both kinds of coffee are made from green coffee beans roasted brown, and both are served black in small cups. The difference is in how they are made. Turkish coffee is boiled in a pot that narrows from the bottom to the top, which intensifies the foaming action during the boiling. The water, coffee, and sugar are mixed according to the individual's preference, and the pot is taken off the fire as soon as the coffee boils. It is put back on at least once to build up a foaming head. Then the coffee is poured into a small cup along with the coffee grounds, which settle at the bottom of the cup. The resulting drink is very thick.

A street-food vendor calls out to customers.

Arab coffee is prepared in a single boil. Sugar is seldom added, and spices such as cloves or cardamom may be added for flavor. Once the coffee boils, it is poured into a second pot without the grounds.

STREET FOOD

Virtually every street corner in Egypt has a stall selling food. Each day millions of people in the big cities will stop on the street to purchase a quick but filling snack. Street stalls are particularly busy at breakfast time. The most popular breakfast is a round, flat bread that has been split open and filled with a spoonful of foul flavored with olive oil and lemon juice. This makes a fast and cheap meal, costing the equivalent of a few cents. Beans are known as "poor man's meat" in Egypt, but foul is an equally popular breakfast for rich Egyptians.

Falafel is another favorite street food. It is made from ground chickpeas with green vegetables mixed with spices, rolled into little balls, and deep fried. Falafel can be eaten on its own or placed inside pita bread. Yogurt, cucumbers, and tomatoes are often added to the sandwich.

Other street vendors sell fried eggplant, stuffed peppers, or baked sweet

Bread forms a central part of the Egyptian diet; people eat it at virtually every meal. Even at a big dinner, there will still be a plate full of bread. Egyptian bread is pita or pocket bread. It is round and flat, about the size of a small dinner plate. The bread is hollow and can be split down the middle and filled with cooked meats or vegetables.

Egyptians eat so much bread that the country has to import wheat to supplement wheat crops grown domestically. Since it is such a big part of the people's diet, the govern-ment subsidizes, or helps to pay for, the cost of bread so that a few cents will buy an armful. With a quarter of Egypt's 84 million people living below the poverty line of $1.65 a day, millions depend on the subsidized bread that sells for less than one U.S. cent per loaf. That is about one-seventh of its market value, or the price it would cost without the government help.

However, the subsidy is a heavy burden on the country's financial resources. When the government tried to raise bread prices in 1977, riots broke out in Cairo. More recently, in 2011, when Egyptians took to the streets to protest against President Hosni Mubarak, one of their chants was: "Bread, freedom, and social justice." And in 2012, newly-elected President Mohamed Morsi's administration decided to work toward cutting out the subsidy on bread altogether. To begin, the government cut the ration to three loaves per person per day, and the size and quality of the loaves were decreased. When people complained, government officials advised them to eat less. At the same time, Morsi cut down on wheat imports, causing a wheat shortage. After Morsi was forced out of office, one of the first tasks facing the new government was how to solve the problem of bread.

potatoes. In the villages, or in the neighborhoods in Cairo, the vendors usually operate late into the night, their stalls lit by kerosene lamps. Some stall owners may even provide chairs for their customers.

Another popular food that people buy on the street is shawarma. This is usually sold from the front of small shops, as more equipment is needed for the preparation of this food. Marinated lamb or chicken slices are stacked one on top of another on a shawarma machine, which consists of a vertical skewer rotating over a charcoal fire. As the skewer rotates, the outer parts of the meat cook first. When a customer comes, the chef slices the meat on the outside and puts the slices into a split round of bread.

A street vendor assembles a sandwich of shawarma from the huge rotating skewer.

INTERNET LINKS

www.foodofegypt.com

Food of Egypt

This is a great source of Egyptian recipes for all occasions and seasons.

www.egypt.cl/typical-food.htm

Egypt Global Culture

Here is a list of popular Egyptian foods.

www.touregypt.net/recipes/

This site offers an archive of recipes from a comprehensive site about Egypt.

SHORBAT ADAS (EGYPTIAN LENTIL SOUP)

Makes 6 to 8 servings

2 Tbsp. olive oil

1 onion, diced

4 garlic cloves, minced

1 large celery rib, diced

1 large carrot, diced

1 large potato, peeled and chopped

1 ¼ cup red lentils

2 quarts (8 cups) vegetable broth

2 tsp. ground cumin

½ tsp. cayenne pepper

¼ tsp. turmeric

2 Tbsp. freshly squeezed lemon juice

salt and freshly ground pepper, to taste

plain yogurt, optional

Heat the oil in a large saucepan over medium heat. Add the onion and garlic and cook until fragrant, about 2 or 3 minutes. Add the celery and carrot and cook for another 5 minutes. Add spices and stir over low heat about 30 seconds. Add the potato, lentils, and vegetable broth. Bring to a boil, then cover and simmer until all the vegetables are very tender, about 40 to 50 minutes.

Puree the soup in batches, using a blender, and return it back to the pot. Add lemon juice. Season with salt and pepper. Serve the soup hot with dollops of yogurt on top and slices of fresh lemon on the side, and include some warm fresh pita bread.

BASBOUSA (SEMOLINA CAKE)

Makes 10 to 12 servings

Syrup

2 cups sugar

2 cups water

1 whole lemon, peeled and juiced

3 tsp. honey

1 tsp. rosewater or orange blossom water
  (optional)

Cake

3 cups semolina

1 cup flour

1 ½ tsp. baking powder

1 cup sugar

1 cup oil

1 cup milk or yogurt

Preheat oven to 350 degrees. Grease a large cookie sheet tray (10 x 16 inches) with oil, butter, or nonstick cooking spray. In a heavy saucepan, bring the sugar, water, lemon juice, and lemon rind to a boil, and boil until the mixture is a runny-syrup consistency. Stir in the honey and rosewater, if using, and set aside.

Mix the semolina, flour, sugar, and baking powder in a large bowl. Add the oil and mix until the batter is well blended. Add the milk or yogurt. Batter will be thick. Add more milk if necessary to spread. Dot the mixture into the greased pan by spoonfuls. Level the top by dipping your hand in milk and smoothing the surface of the batter. Score the batter into even diamonds or squares and place an almond on each piece. Bake at 350 degrees for 30 minutes. Remove the cake from oven and pour the syrup over it. Let it cool.

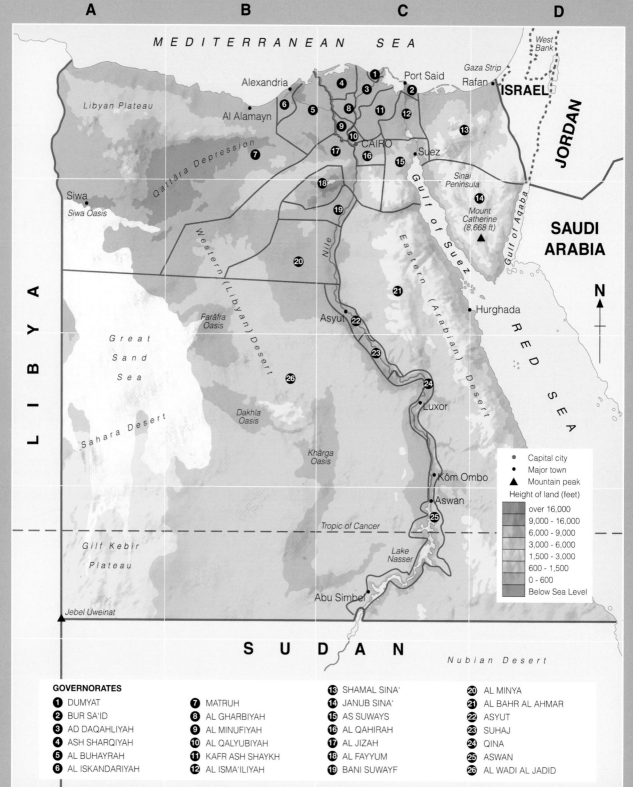

MEDITERRANEAN SEA

Gaza Strip
West Bank
Rafan
ISRAEL

Alexandria
Port Said
Al Alamayn
Libyan Plateau
CAIRO
Suez
Qattâra Depression
Sinai Peninsula
Mount Catherine (8,668 ft) ▲

J O R D A N

SAUDI ARABIA

Siwa
Siwa Oasis

Gulf of Suez
Gulf of Aqaba

Western (Libyan) Desert

Eastern (Arabian) Desert

Nile

Hurghada

R E D   S E A

Farâfra Oasis

G r e a t   S a n d   S e a

Sahara Desert

Dakhla Oasis

Khârga Oasis

Asyut

Luxor

Kôm Ombo

Aswan

L I B Y A

Gilf Kebir Plateau

Tropic of Cancer

Lake Nasser

Jebel Uweinat

Abu Simbel

S U D A N

Nubian Desert

● Capital city
● Major town
▲ Mountain peak
Height of land (feet)
over 16,000
9,000 - 16,000
6,000 - 9,000
3,000 - 6,000
1,500 - 3,000
600 - 1,500
0 - 600
Below Sea Level

N ↑

GOVERNORATES

❶ DUMYAT	
❷ BUR SA'ID	
❸ AD DAQAHLIYAH	
❹ ASH SHARQIYAH	
❺ AL BUHAYRAH	
❻ AL ISKANDARIYAH	

❼ MATRUH
❽ AL GHARBIYAH
❾ AL MINUFIYAH
❿ AL QALYUBIYAH
⓫ KAFR ASH SHAYKH
⓬ AL ISMA'ILIYAH

⓭ SHAMAL SINA'
⓮ JANUB SINA'
⓯ AS SUWAYS
⓰ AL QAHIRAH
⓱ AL JIZAH
⓲ AL FAYYUM
⓳ BANI SUWAYF

⓴ AL MINYA
㉑ AL BAHR AL AHMAR
㉒ ASYUT
㉓ SUHAJ
㉔ QINA
㉕ ASWAN
㉖ AL WADI AL JADID

MAP OF EGYPT

Abu Simbel, C4
Ad Daqahliyah, C1
Al Alamayn, B1
Al Bahr al Ahmar,
    C2—C4, D2—D4
Al Buhayrah,
    A1—B1
Alexandria, B1
Al Fayyum, B1, B2,
    C1, C2
Al Gharbiyah, C1
Al Ghardaqah, C2
Al Iskandariyah, B1
Al Isma'iliyah, C1
Al Jizah, B1, B2, C1,
    C2
Al Minufiyah, C1
Al Minya, B2, C2
Al Qahirah, C1
Al Qalyubiyah, C1
Al Wadi al Jadid,
    A2—A4
Aqaba, Gulf of, D2
Arabian Desert,
    C2—C3, D2—D3
Ash Sharqiyah,
    B1—C1
As Suways, C1—C2
Aswan
    (governorate),
    C3—C4
Aswan (city), C4
Asyut
    (governorate),
    C2—C3
Asyut (city), C2

Bani Suwayf,
    B2—C2
Bur Sa'id, C1

Cairo, C1

Dakhla Oasis, B3
Dumyat, C1

Eastern Desert, see
    Arabian Desert

Farâfra Oasis,
    B2—B3

Gaza Strip, D1
Gilf Kebir Plateau,
    A4
Great Sand Sea,
    A2—A3, B2—B3

Israel, D1

Janub Sina', C1, C2,
    D1, D2
Jebel Uweinat, A4
Jordan, D1—D2

Kafr ash Shaykh,
    C1
Khârga Oasis,
    B3—C3
Kôm Ombo, C3

Lake Nasser, C4
Libya, A1—A5

Libyan Desert,
    B2—B3
Libyan Plateau, A1
Luxor, C3

Matruh, A1, A2, B1,
    B2
Mediterranean Sea,
    A1—D1
Mount Catherine,
    D2

Nile, C1—C5
Nubian Desert, C4,
    C5, D4, D5

Port Said, C1

Qattâra
    Depression, A1,
    A2, B1, B2
Qina, C3—C4

Rafan, D1
Red Sea, D2—D4

Sahara desert,
    A3—A4
Saudi Arabia,
    D1—D3
Shamal Sina',
    C1—D1
Sinai Peninsula, C1,
    C2, D1, D2
Siwa, A2
Siwa Oasis, A2
Sudan, A4—D4,
    A5—D5
Suez, C1
Suez, Gulf of,
    C1—C2
Suhaj, C3

Tropic of Cancer,
    A4—D4

West Bank, D1
Western Desert,
    see Libyan Desert

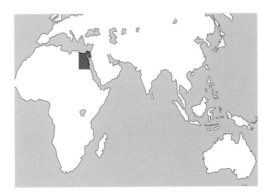

ECONOMIC EGYPT

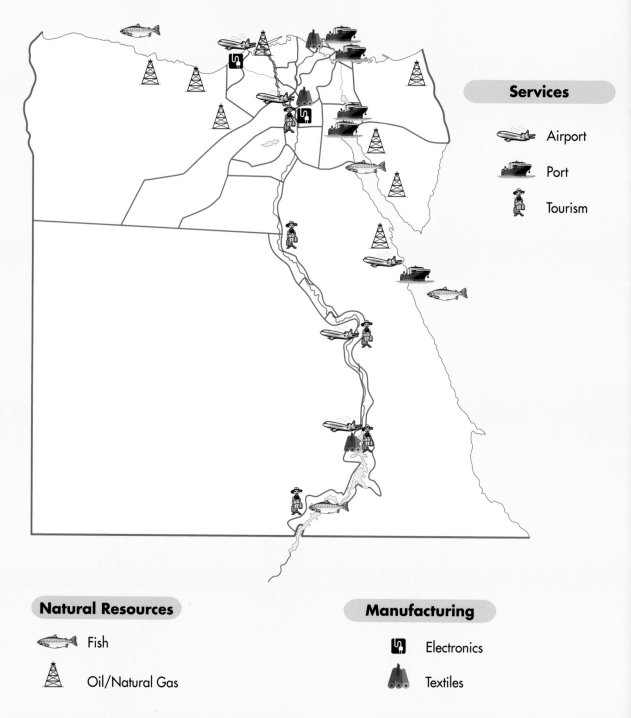

Services

Airport
Port
Tourism

Natural Resources

Fish
Oil/Natural Gas

Manufacturing

Electronics
Textiles

ABOUT THE ECONOMY

OVERVIEW

From 2004 to 2008, the Egyptian government implemented economic reforms to attract foreign investment. However, despite Egypt's economic growth in recent years, living conditions for the average Egyptian remained poor. That helped to cause public discontent. Political uncertainty continues and has significantly slowed down economic growth. Tourism, manufacturing, and construction have been among the hardest hit sectors of the Egyptian economy. Economic growth is likely to remain slow until the political situation in the country stabilizes.

NATURAL RESOURCES

Crude oil, natural gas, asbestos, gypsum, limestone, iron ore, lead, zinc

LAND AREA

384,345 square miles (995,450 square km)

CURRENCY

1 Egyptian pound (EGP) = 100 piasters
Notes: 1, 5, 10, 20, 50, 100 pounds; 25, 50 piasters
Coins: 5, 10, 25 piasters
USD 1 = EGP 6.96 (February 2014)

INFLATION RATE

7.1 percent (2012)

LABOR FORCE

27 million (2010)

LABOR FORCE BY OCCUPATION

Agriculture 29 percent, industry 22 percent, services 49 percent

UNEMPLOYMENT RATE

24.8 percent (2010)
male: 14.7 percent
female: 54.1 percent

AGRICULTURAL PRODUCTS

Beans, corn, cotton, fruit, rice, vegetables, wheat

INDUSTRIAL PRODUCTS

Cement, chemicals, food products, metal products, petroleum products, textiles

MAJOR EXPORTS

Chemicals, cotton, crude oil, metal products, petroleum products, textiles

MAJOR IMPORTS

Chemicals, fuels, machinery, wheat and other food products, wood products

MAJOR TRADE PARTNERS

United States, Italy, Germany, countries in Asia and the Middle East

MAJOR PORTS

Alexandria, Aswan, Asyut, Damietta, Matruh, Port Said, Suez

CULTURAL EGYPT

Greco-Roman Museum
Alexandria's Greco-Roman Museum, founded in 1892, exhibits ancient Greek and Roman art in Egypt, including sculptures of Alexander the Great, Cleopatra, and the Egyptian bull god, Apis. The city also has the country's only Roman Amphitheater.

Cairo Opera House
Cairo's opera house presents various performing arts companies such as the Cairo Symphony Orchestra. Cairo is Egypt's cultural heartbeat—here medieval and modern blend, with hundreds of historical mosques and a media production city.

Great Pyramids
Three pyramids stand together at Giza, but only the Great Pyramid of Khufu is considered one of the Seven Wonders of the Ancient World.

Monastery of the Holy Virgin Mary
According to tradition the Monastery of the Holy Virgin Mary near the city of El-Minya is located on the route that the Holy Family took while fleeing Herod. Many believe that the church was built in the first century CE, making it one of the oldest Christian churches in Egypt.

Great Sand Sea
Led by experienced guides, adventurous tourists visit the Great Sand Sea to see giant dunes. One of the mysteries of these dunes are natural silica glass shards scattered across the southern sands.

Mount Sinai
Many people visit the southern Sinai to climb the mountain where the Bible says God gave Moses the Ten Commandments. Also located in the area is Saint Catherine's Monastery, built in the sixth century CE. It houses Arab, Greek, and Russian works of art and the second largest collection (after the Vatican's) of illuminated manuscripts.

Valley of the Kings and Queens
The tombs of the kings and queens of the New Kingdom were carved into the sides of the Nile valley to keep their treasures safe from tomb raiders. Luxor is home to many more of Egypt's dynastic monuments, such as the Temple of Amon at Karnak and the Temple of Luxor built by Amenhotep III and Ramesses II.

Temple of Ramesses II
The famous temple at Abu Simbel was carved out of sandstone cliffs near the border with Sudan, but had to be moved to higher ground during the building of the Aswan High Dam. There is another temple, dedicated to Ramesses's wife Nefertari.

Felucca Heaven
Feluccas sailing on the Nile at Aswan, where the river flows from Lake Nasser, make a pretty sight at sunset.

ABOUT THE CULTURE

OFFICIAL NAME
Arab Republic of Egypt

CAPITAL
Cairo

OTHER MAJOR CITIES
Al Mansura, Alexandria, Aswan, Asyut, Beni Suwaif, Damietta, Isma'ilia, Luxor, Port Said, Suez, Tanta

GOVERNMENT
A republic, with a president and a prime minister supported by a cabinet of ministers, a legislature, and a judiciary.

NATIONAL FLAG
The red band represents the pre-revolution era, the white band the advent of the revolution, and the black band the end of British occupation. The national emblem, in the middle band, consists of a shield on the breast of an eagle above a scroll with Egypt's Arabic name.

NATIONAL ANTHEM
"My Homeland, My Homeland, My Homeland" (adopted 1979) Lyrics by Mohammad Younis-al Qadi, music by Sayed Darwish. (To listen, go to www.nationalanthems.info/eg.htm.)

POPULATION
85,294,400 (2013)

LIFE EXPECTANCY
73.19 (2013)

AGE STRUCTURE (2013)
0—14 years: 32.3 percent
15—24 years: 18 percent
25—54 years: 38.3 percent
55—64 years: 6.6 percent
65 years and over: 4.8 percent

LANGUAGES
Arabic (official), English, French

LITERACY RATE
73.9 percent (2012)

INTERNET USERS
20.1 million (2009)

ETHNIC GROUPS
Ethnic Egyptian, Bedouin, and Amazigh 99 percent; Nubian, European, and other 1 percent

RELIGIOUS GROUPS
Muslim 90 percent, Coptic Christian 9 percent, other 1 percent

TIMELINE

IN EGYPT	IN THE WORLD
5th millennium BCE	
First settlers in the Nile delta	
2925 BCE	
First pharaonic dynasty is established.	
2780 BCE	
First pyramid is built for King Djoser.	**753 BCE.**
	Rome is founded.
332 BCE	**116–17 BCE**
Alexander the Great invades Egypt.	Roman empire reaches its greatest extent,
51–30 BCE	under Emperor Trajan (98-17).
Reign of Cleopatra VII, the last pharaoh	
395 CE	
Start of Byzantine rule	**600 CE**
639	Height of Mayan civilization
Arabs introduce Islam.	
973	**1000**
Fatimids establish Cairo as the capital.	Chinese perfect gunpowder and
1250	begin to use it in warfare.
Mamluk rule begins.	
1517	**1530**
Egypt becomes part of the Ottoman empire.	Beginning of trans-Atlantic slave trade organized
	by the Portuguese in Africa.
	1558–1603
	Reign of Elizabeth I of England
	1620
	Pilgrims sail the *Mayflower* to America.
	1776
	U.S. Declaration of Independence
	1789–1799
1798	French Revolution
Napoleon Bonaparte invades Egypt.	**1861**
1869	U.S. Civil War begins.
Suez Canal is opened.	
1882	
British begin to colonize Egypt.	**1914**
1936	World War I begins.
Farouk I becomes king.	**1939**
	World War II begins.
1952	
Revolution turns Egypt into a republic.	

IN EGYPT	IN THE WORLD
1956 Gamal Abdel Nasser becomes president.	**1957** Russians launch Sputnik.
	1966–1969 Chinese Cultural Revolution
1967 Israeli troops take the Sinai.	
1970 President Nasser dies; Anwar al-Sadat becomes president.	
1979 Egypt and Israel sign a peace treaty; Israeli troops withdraw from the Sinai.	
1981 President Sadat is assassinated; Hosni Mubarak becomes president.	**1986** Nuclear power disaster at Chernobyl in Ukraine
1989 Egypt rejoins the Arab League.	
1991 Egypt joins the international alliance to expel Iraq from Kuwait.	**1991** Break-up of the Soviet Union
	2001 Al Qaida terrorists attack the United States on September 11.
	2003 War in Iraq begins.
2011 President Mubarak forced from office. "Arab Spring" uprisings sweep through Middle East, culminating in Egypt's January 25 Revolution.	**2011** Tsunami hits Japan, killing more than 15,000 and triggering a nuclear meltdown at a power plant.
2012 In Egypt's first free presidential election, voters elect Mohamed Morsi of the Muslim Brotherhood.	
2013 President Morsi forced from office by the Egyptian military. New interim president Adly Mansour installed.	**2013** Argentine cleric Jorge Bergoglio becomes Pope Francis I, head of the Roman Catholic Church.
2014 Egyptian voters approve new constitution. Deposed President Morsi put on trial.	**2014** The Crimea votes to secede from Ukraine and join Russia.

GLOSSARY

abaya
Long robe worn by Muslim women

ankh
Ancient symbol of life

fellahin
Peasants

felucca
A long, narrow vessel propelled by oars or sails or both.

galabia (GEH-lah-bia)
An ankle-length outfit with long sleeves worn by men in the countryside

hajj
The pilgrimage to Mecca

hijab
Veil worn by Muslim women

ihram (EE-rahm)
White clothing worn by male pilgrims while performing the hajj

imam
The religious or prayer leader at a mosque

Ka'bah (KAH-AH-bah)
The central shrine of Islam located in the center of the Grand Mosque in Mecca; the focal point for daily prayer and the hajj

khedive (kai-DEV)
The name given to the Turkish governor of Egypt from 1867 to 1914

mahr (MAHR)
Money that the groom gives to the bride's father

mazoun (MAA-zoon)
A government witness at a wedding

muezzin
The mosque official who calls to prayer

oasis
A fertile spot in the desert watered by a spring, stream, or well

papyrus
A water reed, common in ancient Egypt, used for making paper

pharaoh
Egypt's ancient kings

pharaonic
Of, or relating to, the pharaohs or their times

pharaonism
An ideology that looks to Egypt's pre-Islamic past for a national identity apart from its Arab identity; a national spirit based on Egypt's ancient heritage

shariah (SHA-ri-ah)
Islamic law

Sunni
One of two major divisions in Islam (the other is Shia). Sunni Muslims make up about 85 percent of the world's Muslims.

surah (SOO-rah)
A chapter of the Qur'an

To Bedawi (TOW BAY-dah-wee)
A language spoken in the Eastern Desert

wadi (wah-DEE)
An ancient desert valley that was once a riverbed

FOR FURTHER INFORMATION

BOOKS

Biesty, Stephen and Stewart Ross. *Egypt: In Spectacular Cross-Section*. New York: Oxford University Press, 2005.

Boyer, Crispin. *National Geographic Kids Everything Ancient Egypt: Dig Into a Treasure Trove of Facts, Photos, and Fun*. Washington, D.C.: National Geographic Children's Books, 2012

Hart, George. *DK Eyewitness Books: Ancient Egypt*. New York: DK Publishing, Inc., 2008

Hawass, Zahi. *Tutankhamun and the Golden Age of the Pharaohs*. Washington, D.C.: National Geographic, 2005.

Mehdawy, Magda. *My Egyptian Grandmother's Kitchen: Traditional Dishes Sweet and Savory*. New York: The American University in Cairo Press, 2006.

Metropolitan Museum of Art and Catharine Roehrig. *Fun with Hieroglyphs*. New York: Simon & Schuster Books for Young Readers, 2008.

Osman, Tarek. *Egypt on the Brink: From Nasser to the Muslim Brotherhood, Revised and Updated, third edition*. New Haven: Yale University Press, 2013.

Riolo, Amy. *Nile Style: Egyptian Cuisine and Culture: Expanded Edition*, New York: Hippocrene Books, 2013.

WEBSITES

Ancient Egypt. www.ancientegypt.co.uk

Bibliotheca Alexandrina (The New Library of Alexandria). www.bibalex.org

Central Intelligence Agency World Factbook. www.cia.gov/library/publications/the-world-factbook/geos/eg.html

Egypt State Information Service. www.sis.gov.eg

Lonely Planet World Guide: Destination Egypt. www.lonelyplanet.com/egypt

Ministry of State for Environmental Affairs. www.eeaa.gov.eg

Tour Egypt: The Complete Guide to Ancient and Modern Egypt. www.touregypt.net

The World Bank Group. www.worldbank.org/en/country/egypt

World Travel Guide: Egypt. www.travel-guide.com/data/egy/egy.asp

VIDEOS

Egypt: Secrets of the Pharaohs. National Geographic, 1998. (VHS)

Egypt's Golden Empire. Warner Home Video, 2002. (DVD)

Mystery of the Sphinx—Expanded Edition. UFO TV, 2007. (DVD)

BIBLIOGRAPHY

BOOKS

Asante, Molefi K. *Culture and Customs of Egypt*. Westport, CT: Greenwood, 2002.

Baines, John et al. *Religion in Ancient Egypt: Gods, Myths, and Personal Practice*. Ithaca: Cornell University Press, 1991.

Diamond, Arthur. *Egypt, Gift of the Nile*. New York: Dillon Press, 1992.

El Mahdy, Christine. *Mummies, Myth and Magic in Ancient Egypt*. New York: Thames and Hudson, 1989.

Hopwood, Derek. *Egypt: Politics and Society*, 1945–1990. London: Harper Collins Academic, 1991.

Murphy, Caryle. *Passion for Islam: Shaping the Modern Middle East: The Egyptian Experience*. Scribner, 2002.

Okijk, Pamela. *The Egyptians*. Columbus: Silver Burdett Press, 1989.

Shaw, Ian. *The Oxford History of Ancient Egypt*. Oxford: Oxford University Press, 2000.

Silverman, David P. *Ancient Egypt*. Oxford: Oxford University Press, 1997.

WEBSITES

Al Jazeera America: Egypt News. www.aljazeera.com

Ancient History Encyclopedia: Egyptian Culture. www.ancient.eu.com/Egyptian_Culture

Arab Republic of Egypt Ministry of Petroleum. www.petroleum.gov.eg/en/AboutEgypt

BBC News: Africa. Egypt Profile. www.bbc.com/news/world-africa-13313370

British Museum: Ancient Egypt. www.ancientegypt.co.uk/menu.html

CIA World Factbook: Egypt. www.cia.gov/library/publications/the-world-factbook/geos/eg.html

Egypt Travel: Egypt's Official Tourism Website. www.egypt.travel

Egyptian Embassy, Washington, D.C. www.egyptembassy.net

Infoplease: Egypt. www.infoplease.com/country/egypt.html

New York Times: World. Egypt News—Revolution and Aftermath. topics.nytimes.com/top/news/international/countriesandterritories/egypt

Smarthistory, Kahn Academy: Ancient Egypt. smarthistory.khanacademy.org/ancient-egypt1.html

State Information Service of Egypt. www.sis.gov.eg/En

Tour Egypt. www.touregypt.net

INDEX

INDEX